KOREAN LANGUAGE for Beginners

LEARN Korean
LANGUAGE WORKBOOK FOR BEGINNERS

- ✓ Master the Hangul Alphabet, Step-by-Step
- ✓ Understand How to Read, Write & Speak Korean
- ✓ Detailed Sound and Pronunciation Guides
- ✓ Stroke Order Diagrams and Writing Tips
- ✓ Learn with Writing Exercises & Quizzes

POLYSCHOLAR

www.polyscholar.com

© Copyright 2021 Jennie Lee - All Rights Reserved

© Copyright 2021 Jennie Lee - All Rights Reserved

Legal Notice: This book is copyright protected. This book is only for personal use. The content contained within this book may not be reproduced, duplicated or transmitted without direct written permission from the author or the publisher. You cannot amend, distribute, sell, use, quote or paraphrase any part of the content within this book, without the consent of the author or publisher.

CONTENTS

1. Introduction — 4
   - How to use this book — 4
   - Background Information — 5
   - Getting Started — 8
   - About Syllables & Rules — 10
   - Writing Tips — 12
2. Learn the Basic Hangul — 16
3. Revision & Practice — 41
4. Compound Letters — 49
5. Complex & Final Consonants — 77
6. Pronunciation & Sound Changes — 89
7. Useful Words & Vocabulary — 101
8. Reference Charts & Answers — 123
9. Extra Practice Pages — 129
10. Flash Cards — 142

Tip: *This book works best with gel pens, pencils, biros and similar media. Take care with markers and ink, as heavy or wet media may result in paper bleed or transfer through to the pages below. Here are some test boxes to check how suitable your pens will be:*

HOW TO USE THIS BOOK

One of the fastest ways to learn and understand any new foreign language is repetition. As you progress through this book, you will find spaces on the page to practice what you learn, with a range of writing exercises a quick quiz at the end of each section.

Later in the book, there are more advanced writing drills and some useful vocabulary further develop your new-found Hangul knowledge. This book has been designed to be scribbled written in but feel free to photocopy pages *(for personal use)* if you would rather work on your writing separately.

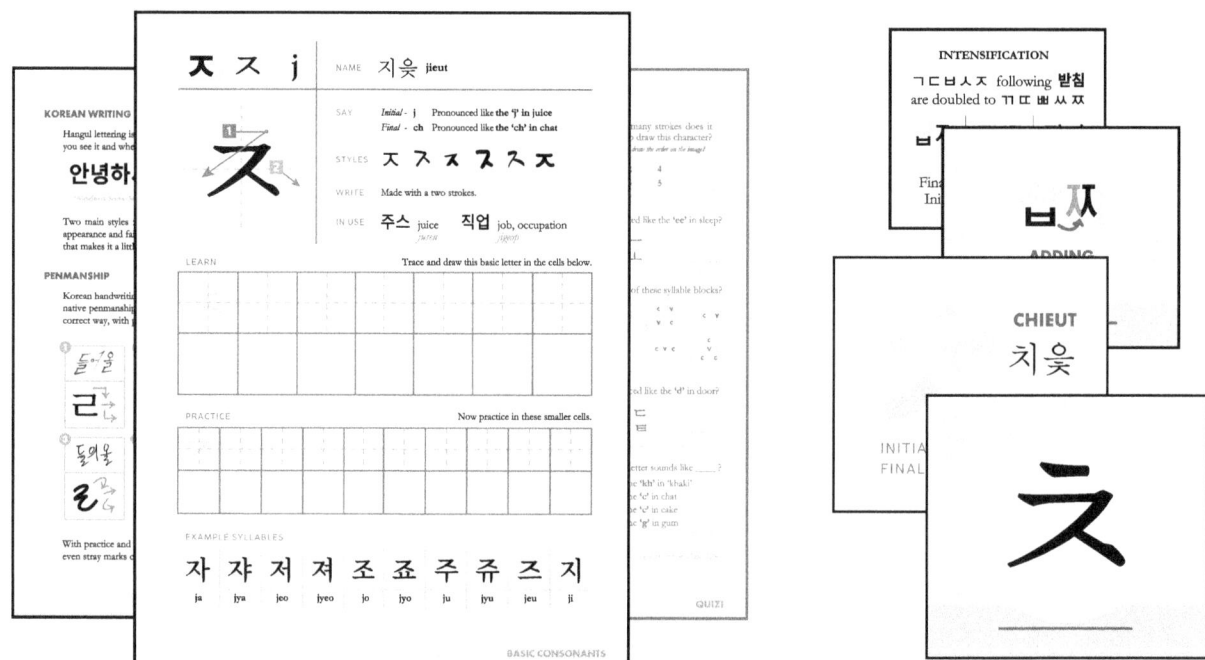

LEARN, MEMORIZE, AND PRACTICE YOUR HANGUL   **FLASHCARD PAGES INCLUDED!**

We have included additional pages with practice grids that you can use once you have learned how to draw Hangul characters, form syllables, and write words! Again, if it is easier, you can copy those for use at home.

The final part of this workbook contains a set of flashcard style pages that can either be photocopied or cut out. They are a great way to help you memorize the symbols and test your knowledge. *Younger learners should seek help from an adult to cut them out!*

INTRODUCTION

Learning to read, write, and speak Korean might seem like an incredibly daunting task, but we have taken care to create a workbook that will make it **easier and quicker**!

The first hurdle in learning Korean is a big one for English speakers, and that is the Korean alphabet, known as **Hangul**. You have no doubt already seen that it consists of letters that look entirely foreign when compared to western alphabets. Not only must we learn a new language, but it is written in a completely new form of text!

In no time at all, you will see that the Korean language system is much easier to learn than it first looks. This book will teach you all about the Hangul alphabet and, by the end, you will understand how to read, write, and speak Korean! *Pretty nifty, eh?*

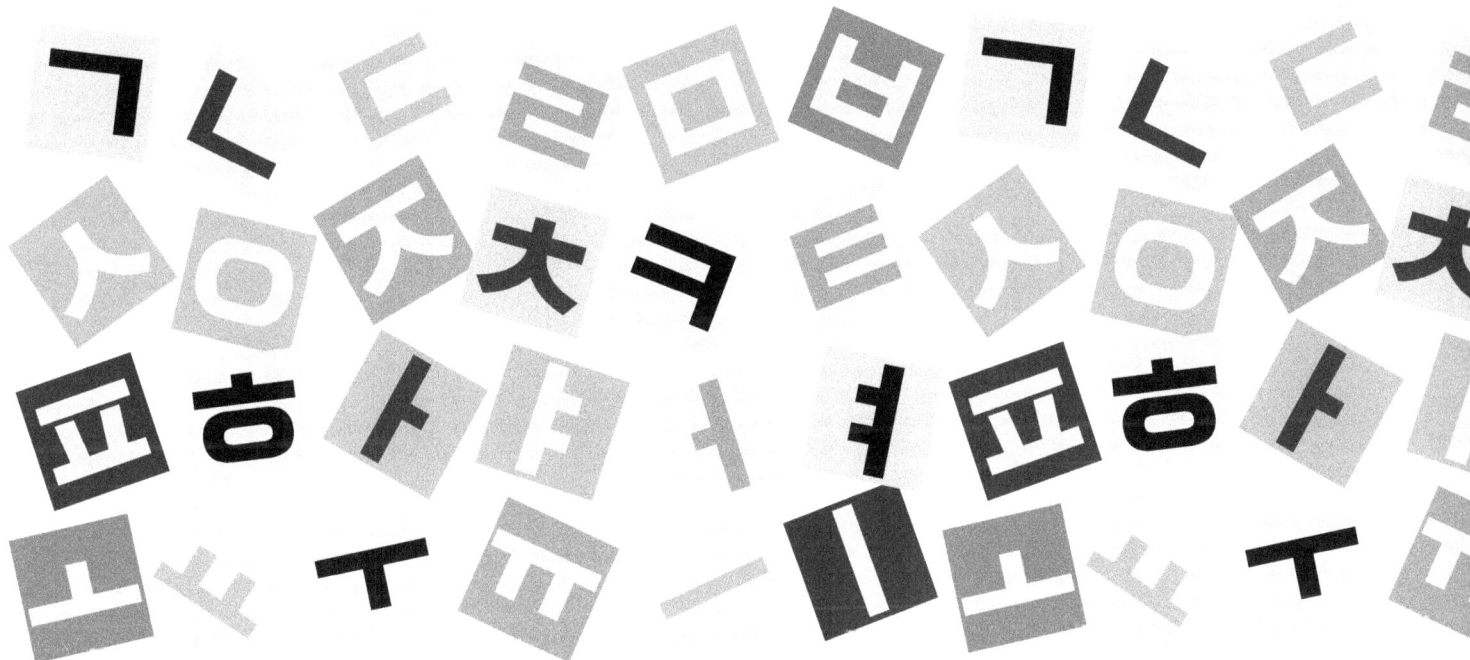

Hangul is the name given to the alphabet and writing system used throughout Korea. The name is composed of two Korean words, **han** (한) and **geul** (글), translating literally as **'great script'**. *Han* can refer to Korea as a whole, so it is also translated as *'Korean Script'*. Hangul is made with **consonants** and **vowels**; only the letters look different!

(BRIEF) HISTORY

Until the *mid-1400s*, Koreans would have written in a mixture of Chinese and ancient, native scripts that were based on phonetics. There were *(and still are)* a vast number of unique Chinese characters that made the language difficult to memorize and use. To do so also required education available only to the wealthy and upper classes, meaning even basic literacy was beyond the poorer and less-privileged lower classes.

To promote and encourage literacy on a much larger scale, **King Sejong the Great** took it upon himself to design a new and unique language system that was simple, logical, and easy to learn...

...the Hangul alphabet that we use today!

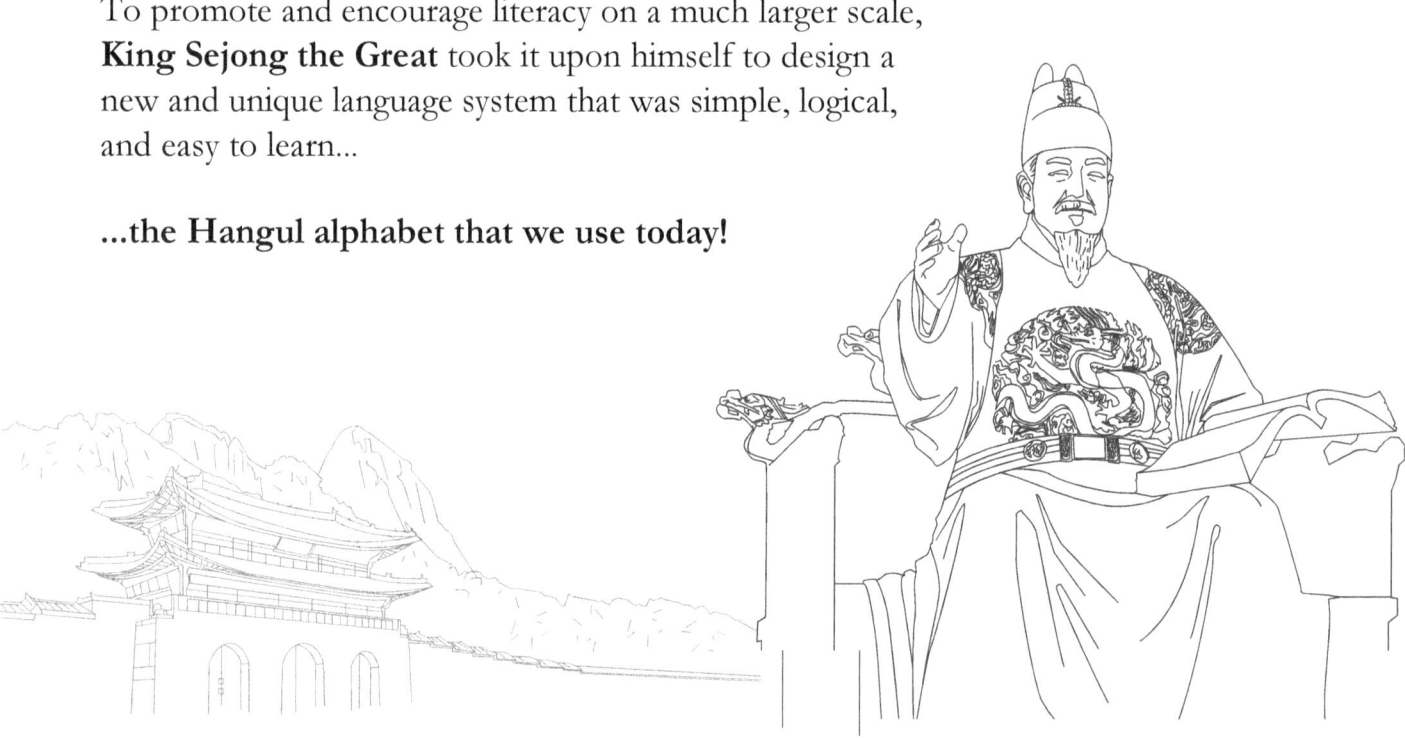

LEARNING KOREAN

When starting to learn Korean, the temptation might be to look up words or phrases for specific scenarios and try and commit how they sound to memory. While that may work in the short term, sooner or later, you will need to read and write using the native script - and must virtually start from scratch again. *There is just no avoiding it!*

Therefore, it is essential to begin by first mastering the Korean alphabet. If you start by simply learning each of the Hangul letters instead of one-off words or phrases, you will find that you can understand all things Korean with ease and much faster!

Introduction

HANGUL IS EASY!

In contrast to Chinese or Japanese, each consisting of *thousands* of unique and complex *Kanji* characters, the Korean language is far simpler:

蔵 儀 遵 帰
Kanji symbols convey entire words or larger chunks of meaning, so they need to be memorized.

한글 (ㅎㅏㄴㄱㅇㅡㄹ)
Korean has a simplified alphabet which is far easier to learn - we read, write, and speak, letter by letter!

Some everyday Chinese Kanji may require up to 15 separate marks to write, while other, less common symbols take anywhere from 20 to 84 strokes to write! The good news for you is that even the most complicated Hangul letters are drawn with only five strokes.

ROMANIZATION

The foreign letters and words that we want to learn must be shown with *romanization* at first - this is where our familiar Latin-based lettering system is used to convey the sounds that each character represents. There are often no equivalent letters for the exact sounds, so it is far from ideal. We will work on memorizing Hangul quickly so that you can avoid *Romanized* translation as soon as possible - *the hard work is going to be worth it, though, trust me!*

It is worth noting that there are several different versions of romanization, each using slightly different letters to the next. The only accurate representation of the sounds is the Hangul alphabet itself, and there is no perfect way to show Korean in English.

PRONUNCIATION

Learning to pronounce Korean well begins when learning Hangul. It is good practice to say words and letters out loud as you learn. Only practice will help you develop a natural and native-sounding accent, and it takes time. We would advise beginning to watch and listen to Korean TV shows with Hangul subtitles once you have a grasp of the alphabet.

Note: This workbook includes basic introductions to pronunciation, but this is inevitably taught more effectively with some audio. Practice pages display close English equivalents using similar-sounding words.

GETTING STARTED

The **Hangul** alphabet consists of just **24 basic letters** that we combine to create all the symbols and characters we need for Korean words. There are only **14 basic consonants** and **10 basic vowels** to learn, so **let us get started**!

BASIC CONSONANTS

The design of basic Hangul consonants was centered around the shapes that are made with the mouth, tongue, throat, and lips when they are articulated and said out loud:

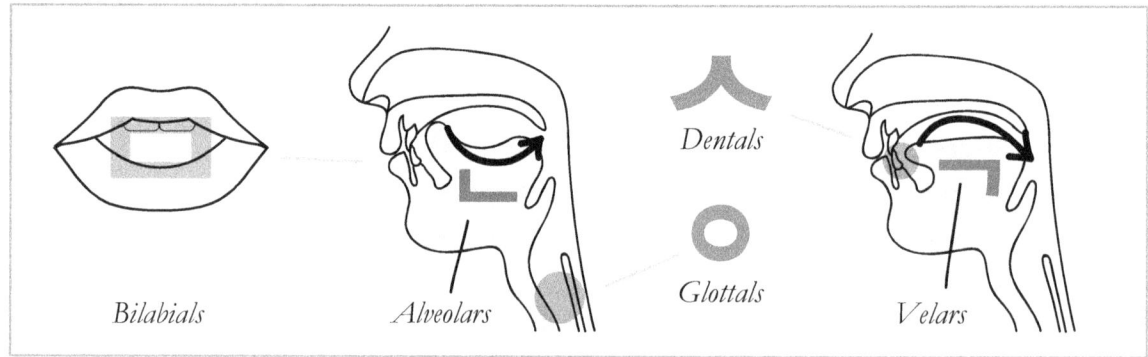

Once the five initial shapes were determined, additional consonant letters were then created by adding extra lines to those first letters. The alphabet is often displayed in a somewhat *alphabetical* order - as that is not important to learn right now, we will **group and arrange letters by shape** to make learning them that little bit **more efficient**:

Hangul	ㄱ	ㅋ	ㄴ	ㄷ	ㅌ	ㅁ	ㄹ
Romanization	g/k	k	n	d/t	t	m	r/l

Hangul	ㅂ	ㅍ	ㅅ	ㅈ	ㅊ	ㅇ	ㅎ
Romanization	b/p	p	s	j/ch	ch	-/ng	h

Note: Hangul has pronunciations that roman letters cannot precisely match, with sounds that change depending on their use.

Basic Hangul

BASIC VOWELS

The basic vowels were designed using shapes that represented the Earth *(Yin)*, the Sky *(Yang)*, and Mankind *(Humans being the Mediator between the two others)*.

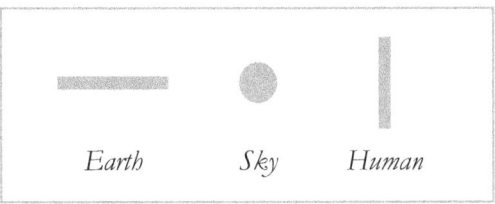

In modern Hangul, the dot representing the heavens *(shown as the sun or a star)* is now joined to the other shapes and has essentially been *replaced* with a short line.

The names of the vowels are like the sounds that they represent. You will notice that some vowels have a taller, '**vertical**' shape *(see table below)* and, the other characters have a flatter shape and a '**horizontal**' orientation:

ㅏ	ㅑ	ㅓ	ㅕ	ㅣ
a	ya	eo	yeo	i

These *'vertical'* vowels are placed directly to the right side of any consonant that precedes them.

ㅗ	ㅛ	ㅜ	ㅠ	ㅡ
o	yo	u	yu	eu

This second group of *'horizontal'* vowels are placed directly below a preceding consonant.

Vowels and consonants do not represent anything on their own - they are **always** combined with at least one of the others. Two or more letters are used to create real syllables and sounds. For example, the letter ㄱ does not have meaning by itself but add the vowel ㅏ and it becomes 가. *(or 'ga' if we Romanize it - sounding like 'gah')*

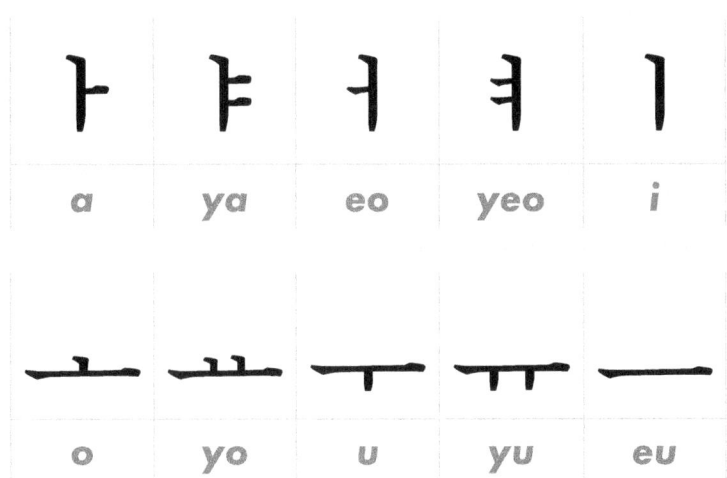

At a minimum, 1 consonant + 1 vowel = 1 syllable

SYLLABLE BLOCKS

Korean words are written and displayed in a series of 'blocks' - each of these blocks will contain a syllable, just like the examples at the bottom of the previous page, and they each represent a sound. These **syllable blocks** are *built* using the individual Hangul letters that encountered before - let us look at an example quickly below:

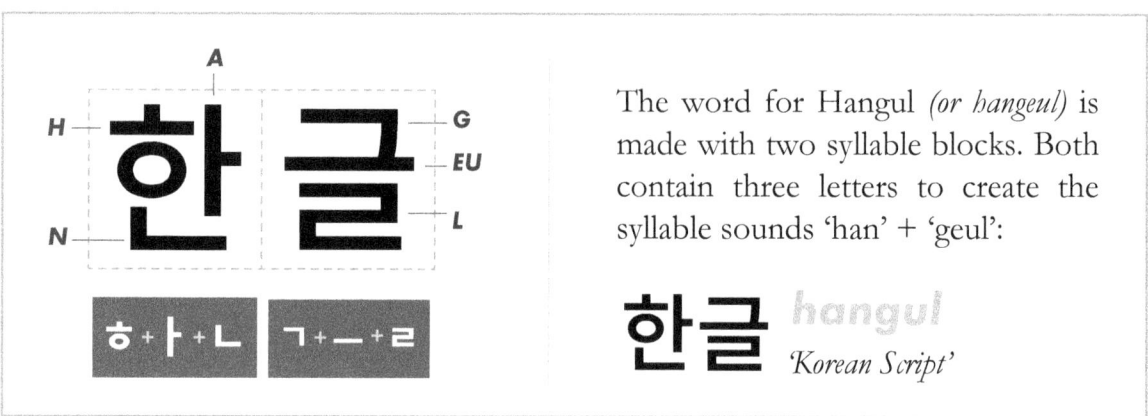

The word for Hangul *(or hangeul)* is made with two syllable blocks. Both contain three letters to create the syllable sounds 'han' + 'geul':

한글 *hangul*
'Korean Script'

A FEW SIMPLE RULES

Once you have learned all the letters and can remember just a few simple rules about using them in blocks, you can basically read and write Korean! *That almost sounds too easy, right?*

① Syllable blocks **always** have a **minimum of two letters.**

② Every syllable **begins with a consonant** and that is **always followed by a vowel.**

③ Each syllable is **written in its own square block.**

④ Letters are *squeezed* or *stretched* to occupy a **similar amount of space** to the others.

There are thousands of possible syllables in theory but *do not let that worry you.* You are not likely to encounter any with more than four letters and, by simply learning the letters first, you will be able to understand every single one of them with ease. This will be how you learned to read and write in your own language - through learning the alphabet and how letters are combined and interact to make syllables and sounds.

Syllables

BUILDING SYLLABLES

The layout of a syllable block is determined by the shape of the vowel and the number of letters inside. Do you remember how vowels have either **vertical** or **horizontal** shapes? Writing from left to right, and top to bottom, syllables start with an **initial consonant** in the left half *(for vertical vowels)* or in the upper half *(for horizontal vowels)*.

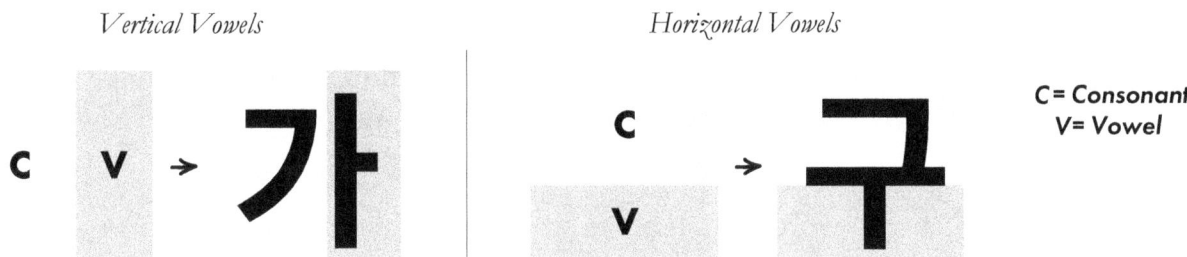

When a third and fourth letter is added to the syllable, they are placed directly underneath the first two, from left to right again. Let's look at some more examples:

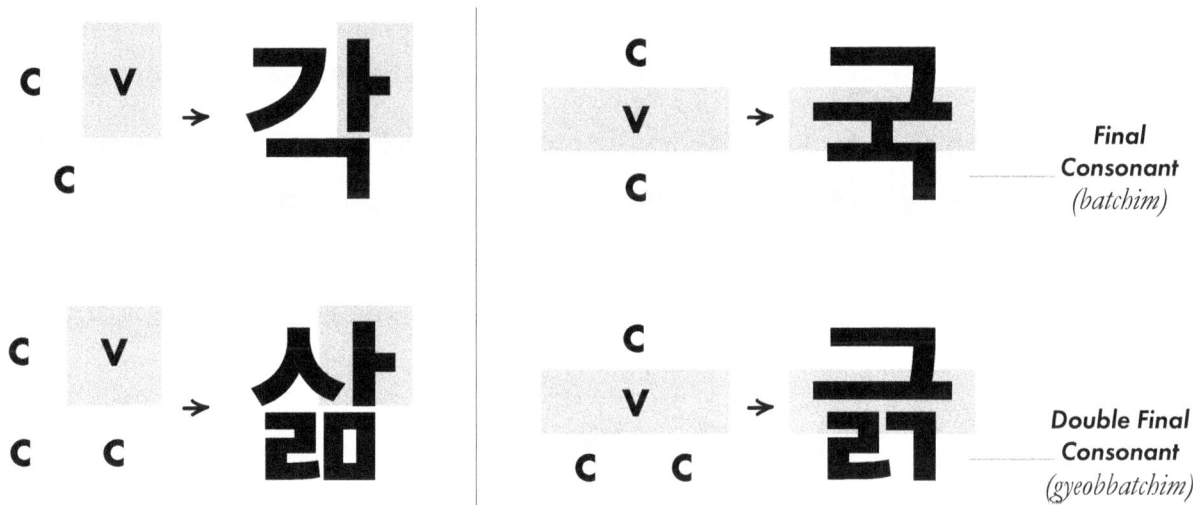

Consonants at the bottom of a syllable are called **batchim** 받침 or *'final consonants'*. They are easier to understand once you have learned more, so *let's keep things simple at this stage...*

Essentially, **batchim** 받침 *(literally meaning 'support')* are a grammatical feature unique to Korean, where consonants carry a different pronunciation at the bottom of a syllable. Vowels are never **batchim**, so the pronunciations you will learn are unaffected here!

IMPORTANT VOWEL RULE

We have learned that every syllable begins with a consonant and has a minimum of two letters - *but what if a block begins with a vowel sound?* This happens quite frequently with 한글 and there is **a critical but easy rule to learn** for solving this problem. While none of the letters are used in isolation, this rule is essential for vowels:

When syllables begin with a vowel, we use consonant ㅇ as a silent placeholder. At the front of a syllable, and as an **initial consonant**, it has no sound. This is an easy rule to memorize - <u>**vowels are never written on their own!**</u>

Here is an example word - the Korean word for alligator - showing this rule in action:

LETTER SHAPES

Some letters can look a little different depending on where they are in a syllable block. The most common example is the letter ㄱ *(called giyeok)*, which gets stretched, squashed, and squeezed quite often - letter shapes are determined by all other letters in the syllable:

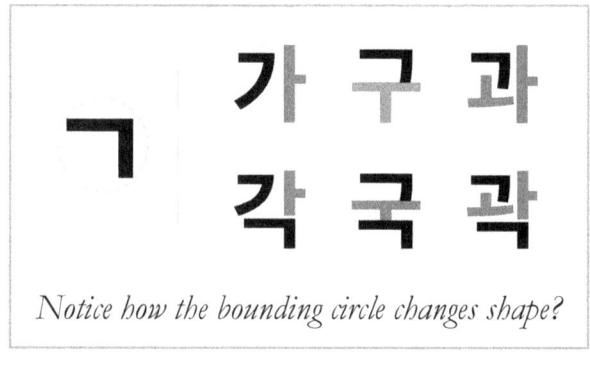

Notice how the bounding circle changes shape?

There are no hard and fast rules for letter shapes, and appearances even vary between handwriting styles. The important thing to remember is that letters are drawn with the same number of strokes, in the same order, and have the same overall form.

The same shape changes occur regardless of font or writing style e.g. ㄱ+ㅣ = **기** 기 and 기. *(Some of the other letters with alternate graphic styles include: ㅈ, ㅊ, ㅉ, ㄹ and ㅎ)*

Writing Tips

READING & WRITING

Korean was once written in the vertical style like other languages from around Asia, such as Chinese or Japanese, but sightings tend to be limited to older, traditional documents. If you do encounter vertical, writing it is likely a graphic design choice, like in signage - just as it is possible to see the odd bit of western text used in a similar way. Most Korean text is written horizontally nowadays.

As we learned when looking at syllables, we write letter by letter, one block at a time - starting at the top left and working towards the lower right. Words are separated with a space, too - *easy huh?*

It makes sense, therefore, that we read left-right and top-bottom too - moving across blocks and words, and sounding out each letter in your head. This becomes quicker and easier with practice. When reaching the end of a syallable, some sounds naturally start to merge with the beginning of any syllables that follow. Then, just like that, you have cracked reading Korean text and how to pronunce it!

STROKE ORDER

Individual Hangul letters and syllables are written in a very specific, step-by-step way that is easy to master. Lines are drawn individually, from top left to bottom right, every time:

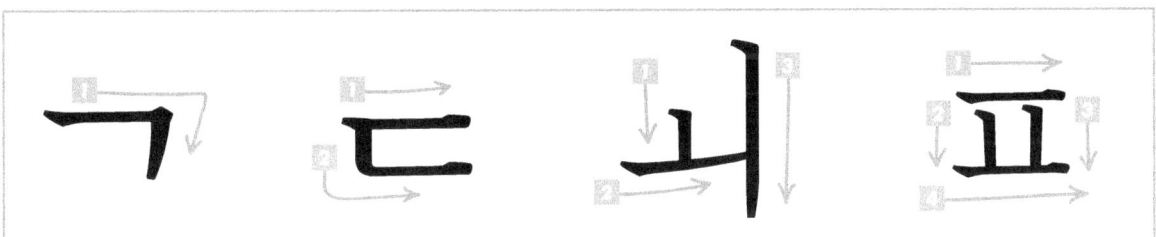

Learning proper stroke order is essential to forming accurate Korean that can be read easily - without the correct stroke order, your writing might be misunderstood entirely. **It is so much easier to learn proper stroke order at the start instead of fixing it later!**

Originally drawn using traditional brushes and ink, every stroke was intentional, creating balanced shapes and highly legible writing. *It was also a very practical way of writing that ensured you did not smudge your text and cover your hands in ink!*

FONTS & APPEARANCE

Hangul lettering is frequently displayed with different appearances, depending on where you see it and whether it has been drawn by hand, printed, or displayed in digital media.

안녕하세요 *'Modern Sans-Serif Style'*   안녕하세요 *'Traditional Serif Style'*

Two main styles feature in this book; a modern *'sans-serif style'* that is blocky in appearance and commonplace; and a more traditional *'serif style'* with an appearance that makes it a little easier to see the stroke order of letters as if individually marked by hand.

PENMANSHIP

Korean handwriting does not need to be perfectly neat - in fact, you will come to see that native penmanship is rarely made with perfectly formed characters! If it is written in the correct way, with proper stroke order, most writing in Hangul can be understood.

If you look at the four handwriting samples displayed on the left, you can see that the same letter ㄹ is drawn differently each time: subsequent examples get less neat, but they are all recognizable.

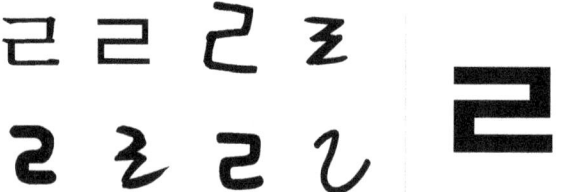

The practice pages in this book feature alternate looking styles for each letter, with handwritten fonts to be used for reference.

With practice and experience, you soon start to notice how a pen has been used and that even stray marks can help you read. *Real Korean handwriting is not all perfect circles and squares!*

ABOUT PRONUNCIATION

One of the most confusing aspects for beginners is the emphasis placed on letters having different pronunciations. Some Hangul are displayed with more than one *roman* letter beside them and usually without any real explanation - *did you notice this on Page 8?* You will learn more about Korean pronunciation later in the book but, for now, here is a brief look at the basics to help you get started:

Different **types of pronunciation** can create different sounds for the same letter - there are a few to be aware of in Korean - **plain**, **voiced**, **aspirated**, or **tensed**:

> **Aspirated/un-aspirated** articulation concerns how much air is pushed out of the mouth when speaking. There is more force *with* aspiration, and we suppress that for un-aspirated sounds. Hold your hand in front of your mouth and say *'chop'* - feel it?

> **Tensed** sounds are more explosive or forceful versions of aspirated sounds.

> **Voiced or voiceless** pronunciation depends on whether you activate the area of your throat that vibrates to affect your speech. Place a finger just above your voice box and then make a long 'sss' sound followed by a long 'zzz' - *did you feel the difference?*

The letters in each column of the table *(below)* are pronounced with increasing force and pitch - each sound becomes a harder and higher version of the one on the previous *'level'*.

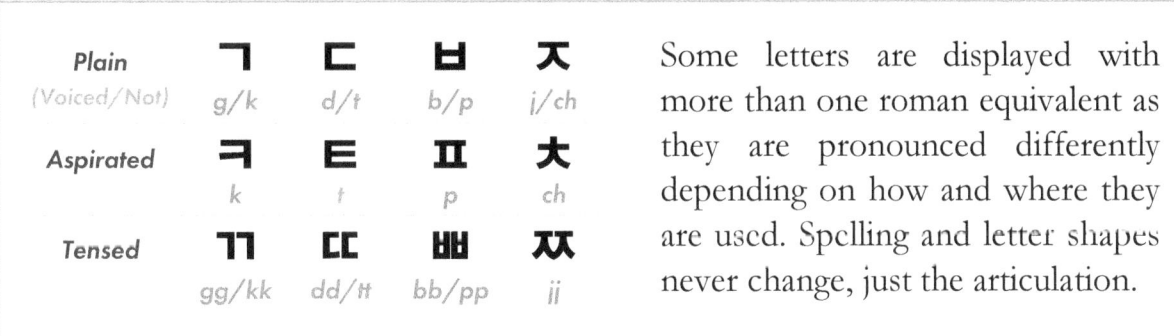

Some letters are displayed with more than one roman equivalent as they are pronounced differently depending on how and where they are used. Spelling and letter shapes never change, just the articulation.

Part of the problem facing students is that *Romanization* is simply not an accurate way to convey the sounds of Hangul. Many consonants sound too similar to each other when romanized, adding an extra layer of difficulty that we cannot avoid. We understand the distinctions between sounds better over time and with more exposure to the language. *Once you have learned about Hangul, we recommend listening to lots of Korean speech!*

Part 2

LEARN THE BASIC HANGUL

ㄱ ㄱ g

NAME 기역 **giyeok**

SAY *Initial* - **g** Pronounced like **the 'g' in gum**
Final - **k** Pronounced like **the 'k' in dock**

STYLES ㄱ ㄱ ㄱ ㄱ ㄱ ㄱ

WRITE Made with a single stroke.

IN USE 개 dog *gae*   가족 family *gajok*

LEARN Trace and draw this basic letter in the cells below.

PRACTICE Now practice in these smaller cells.

EXAMPLE SYLLABLES

가 갸 거 겨 고 교 구 규 그 기
ga gya geo gyeo go gyo gu gyu geu gi

Hangul Consonants

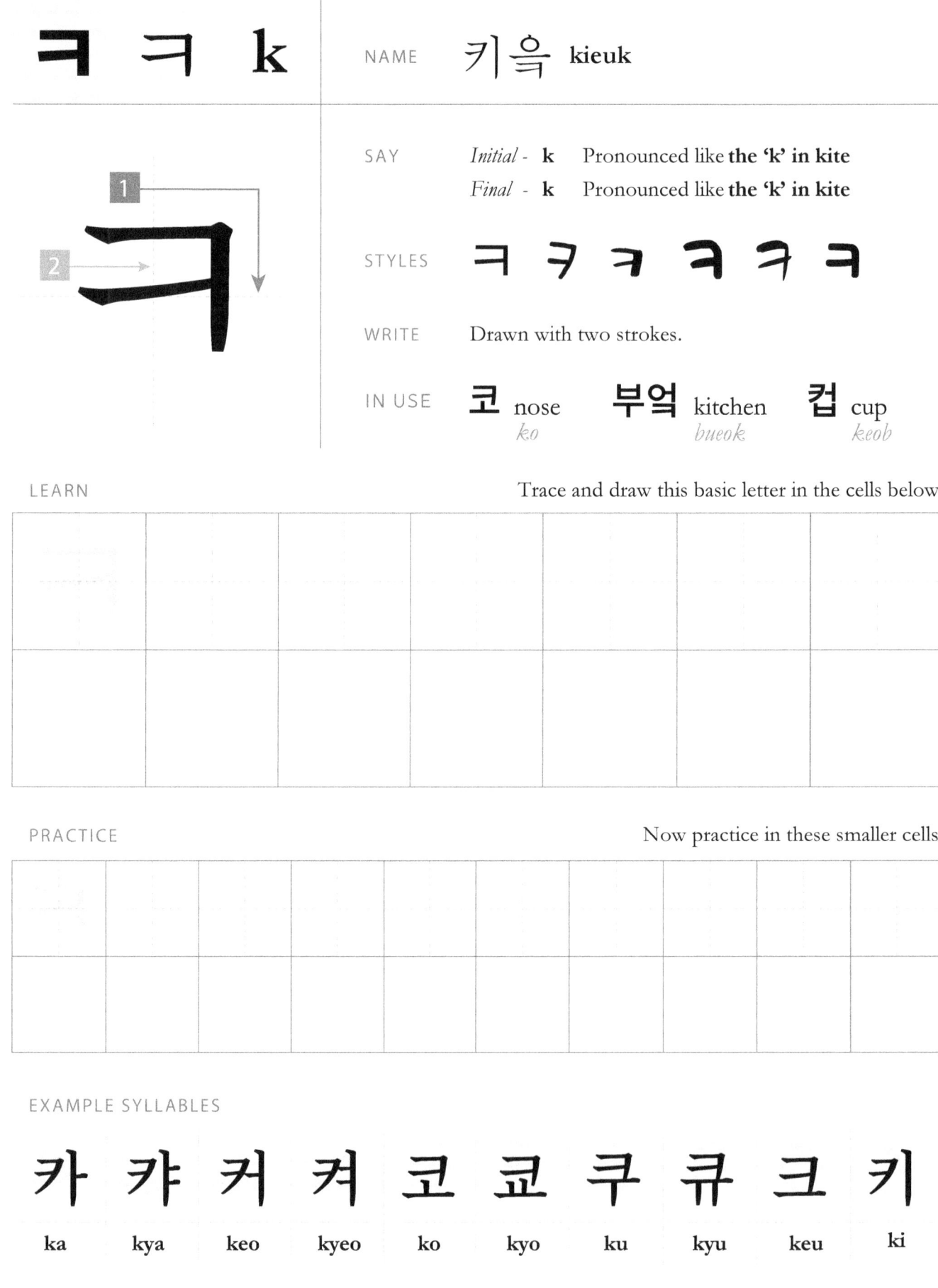

ㅋ ㅋ k

NAME 키읔 kieuk

SAY *Initial* - **k** Pronounced like **the 'k' in kite**
Final - **k** Pronounced like **the 'k' in kite**

STYLES ㅋ ㅋ ㅋ ㅋ ㅋ ㅋ

WRITE Drawn with two strokes.

IN USE 코 nose *ko*   부엌 kitchen *bueok*   컵 cup *keob*

LEARN Trace and draw this basic letter in the cells below.

PRACTICE Now practice in these smaller cells.

EXAMPLE SYLLABLES

카	캬	커	켜	코	쿄	쿠	큐	크	키
ka	kya	keo	kyeo	ko	kyo	ku	kyu	keu	ki

ㄴ ㄴ n

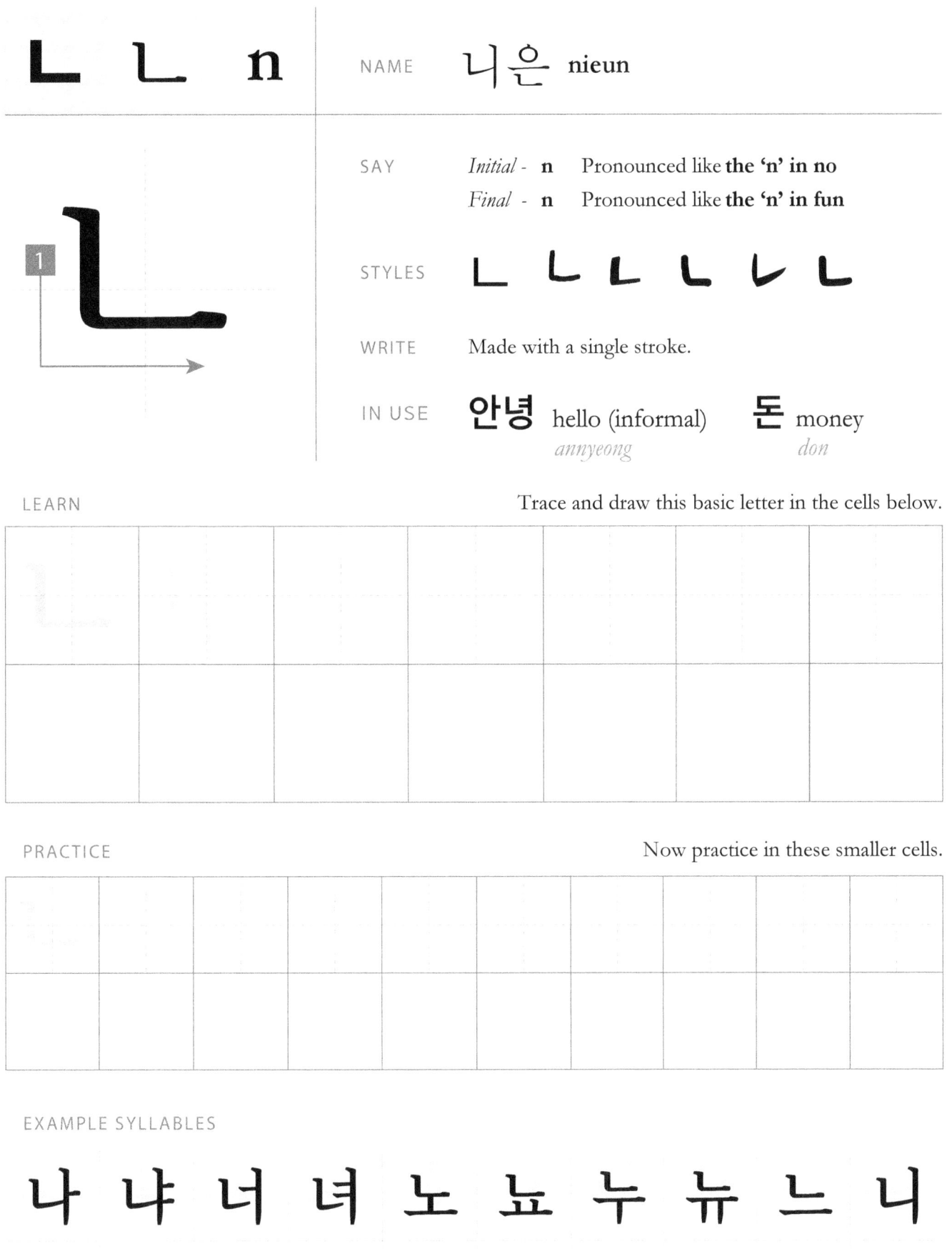

NAME	니은 nieun
SAY	*Initial* - **n** Pronounced like **the 'n' in no** *Final* - **n** Pronounced like **the 'n' in fun**
STYLES	ㄴ ㄴ ㄴ ㄴ ㄴ ㄴ
WRITE	Made with a single stroke.
IN USE	안녕 hello (informal) 돈 money *annyeong* *don*

LEARN

Trace and draw this basic letter in the cells below.

PRACTICE

Now practice in these smaller cells.

EXAMPLE SYLLABLES

나 냐 너 녀 노 뇨 누 뉴 느 니

na nya neo nyeo no nyo nu nyu neu ni

ㄷ ㄷ d

NAME	디귿 digeut
SAY	*Initial* - **d** Pronounced like **the 'd' in door** *Final* - **t** Pronounced like **the 't' in dot**
STYLES	ㄷ ㄷ ㄷ ㄷ ㄷ
WRITE	Made with two strokes.
IN USE	구두 shoes *kudu* 바다 sea, ocean *bada*

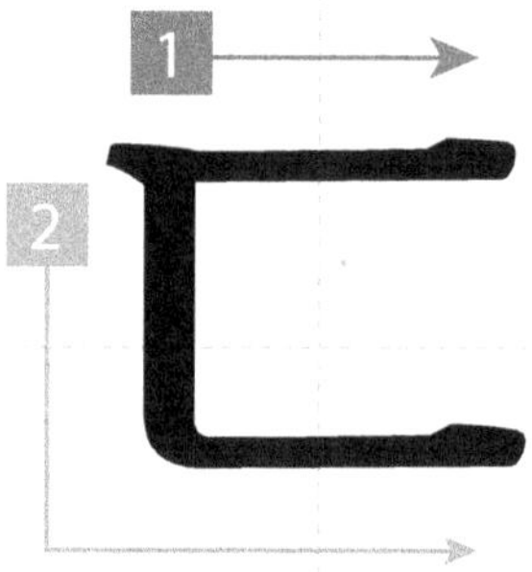

LEARN
Trace and draw this basic letter in the cells below.

PRACTICE
Now practice in these smaller cells.

EXAMPLE SYLLABLES

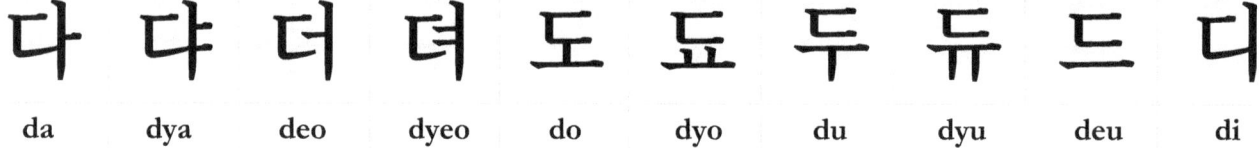

다	댜	더	뎌	도	됴	두	듀	드	디
da	dya	deo	dyeo	do	dyo	du	dyu	deu	di

ㅌ E t

NAME 티읕 tieut

SAY
Initial - **t** Pronounced like **the 't' in tin**
Final - **t** Pronounced like **the 't' in not**

STYLES ㅌ ㅌ ㅌ ㅌ ㅌ

WRITE Made with three strokes.

IN USE 토요일 Saturday 튀김 fried food
toyoil *twigim*

LEARN
Trace and draw this basic letter in the cells below.

PRACTICE
Now practice in these smaller cells.

EXAMPLE SYLLABLES

타 tya 터 텨 토 툐 투 튜 트 티
ta tya teo tyeo to tyo tu tyu teu ti

ㄹ ㄹ r/l

NAME 리을 rieul

SAY *Initial* - **r**   Pronounced like **the 'r' in run**
Final - **l**   Pronounced like **the 'l' in reel**

STYLES ㄹ ㄹ ㄹ ㄹ ㄹ ㄹ

WRITE Drawn with three strokes.

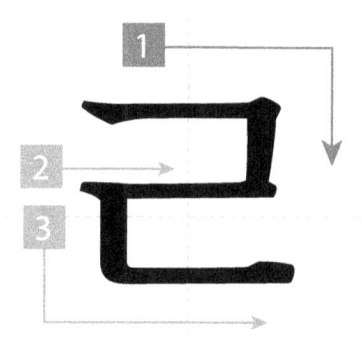

IN USE 라면 ramen noodles   주말 weekend
ramyeon   *jumal*

LEARN

Trace and draw this basic letter in the cells below.

PRACTICE

Now practice in these smaller cells.

EXAMPLE SYLLABLES

라   랴   러   려   로   료   루   류   르   리
ra   rya   reo   ryeo   ro   ryo   ru   ryu   reu   ri

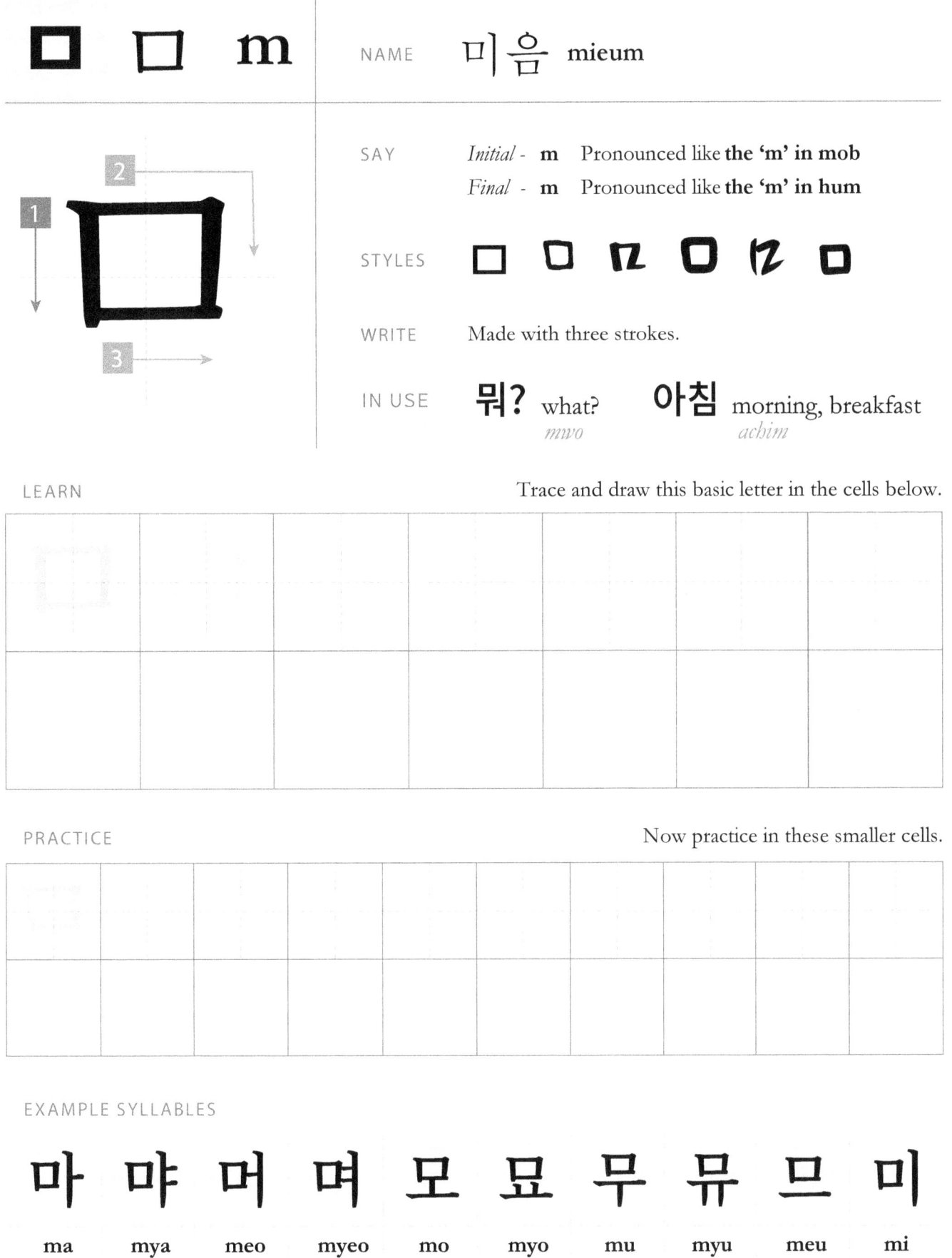

ㅁ ㅁ m

NAME 미음 mieum

SAY
Initial - **m**   Pronounced like **the 'm' in mob**
Final - **m**   Pronounced like **the 'm' in hum**

STYLES ㅁ ㅁ ㄇ ㅁ ㄇ ㅁ

WRITE Made with three strokes.

IN USE 뭐? what?   아침 morning, breakfast
mwo   *achim*

LEARN   Trace and draw this basic letter in the cells below.

PRACTICE   Now practice in these smaller cells.

EXAMPLE SYLLABLES

마 먀 머 며 모 묘 무 뮤 므 미
ma mya meo myeo mo myo mu myu meu mi

ㅂ ㅂ b

NAME 비읍 bieup

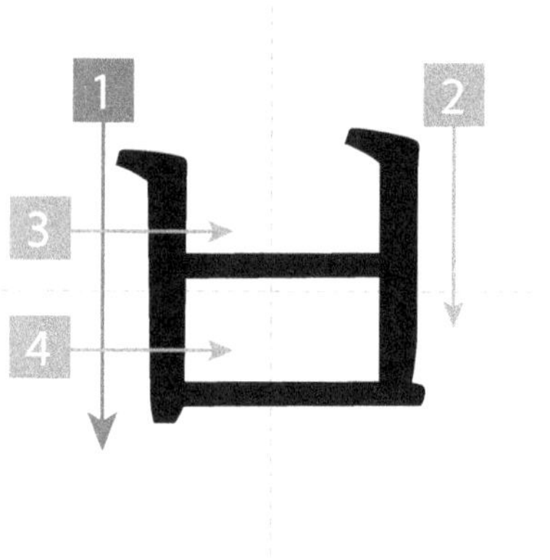

SAY
Initial - **b**   Pronounced like **the 'b' in baby**
Final - **p**   Pronounced like **the 'p' in slap**

STYLES ㅂ ㅂ ㅂ ㅂ ㅂ

WRITE Made with four straight strokes.

IN USE   비 rain   버스 bus   밥 rice
           bi   *beoseu*   *bap*

LEARN
Trace and draw this basic letter in the cells below.

PRACTICE
Now practice in these smaller cells.

EXAMPLE SYLLABLES

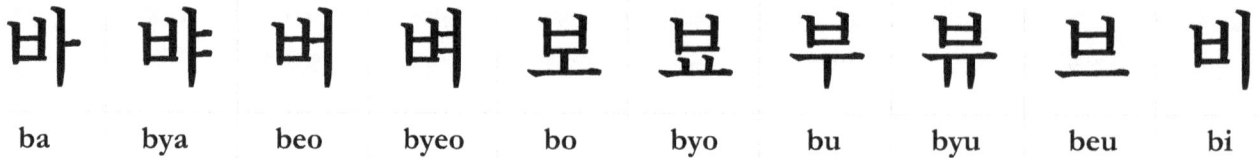

바 byа 버 벼 보 뵤 부 뷰 브 비
ba bya beo byeo bo byo bu byu beu bi

ㅍ ㅍ p

NAME 피읖 pieup

SAY *Initial* - **p** Pronounced like **the 'p' in pizza**
Final - **p** Pronounced like **the 'p' in nap**

STYLES ㅍ ㅍ ㅍ ㅍ ㅍ ㅍ

WRITE Drawn with four strokes.

IN USE 파티 party *pati*   피자 pizza *pija*   커피 coffee *keopi*

LEARN

Trace and draw this basic letter in the cells below.

PRACTICE

Now practice in these smaller cells.

EXAMPLE SYLLABLES

파	퍄	퍼	펴	포	표	푸	퓨	프	피
pa	pya	peo	pyeo	po	pyo	pu	pyu	peu	pi

ㅅ ㅅ s

NAME 시옷 siot

SAY
Initial - s   Pronounced like **the 's' in snow**
Final - t   Pronounced like **the 't' in carpet**
Note: Sometimes 'sh-', see p.98

STYLES ㅅ ㅅ ㅅ ㅅ ㅅ ㅅ

WRITE Drawn with two strokes.

IN USE 시 poem, city   야자수 palm tree
           si   *yajasu*

LEARN
Trace and draw this basic letter in the cells below.

PRACTICE
Now practice in these smaller cells.

EXAMPLE SYLLABLES

사 샤 서 셔 소 쇼 수 슈 스 시

sa sya seo syeo so syo su syu seu si

ㅈ ᄌ j

NAME	지읒 jieut
SAY	*Initial* - **j** Pronounced like **the 'j' in juice**
	Final - **t** Pronounced like **the 't' in chat**
STYLES	ㅈ ㅈ ㅈ ㅈ ㅈ ㅈ
WRITE	Made with two strokes.
IN USE	주스 juice 직업 job, occupation
	juseu *jigeop*

LEARN

Trace and draw this basic letter in the cells below.

PRACTICE

Now practice in these smaller cells.

EXAMPLE SYLLABLES

자 쟈 저 져 조 죠 주 쥬 즈 지
ja jya jeo jyeo jo jyo ju jyu jeu ji

NAME	치읓 chieut
SAY	*Initial* - **ch** Pronounced like **the 'ch' in chat** *Final* - **t** Pronounced like **the 't' in cat**
STYLES	大 ㅊ ㅊ ㅊ ㅊ 大
WRITE	Drawn with three strokes.
IN USE	차 car *cha* 부츠 boots *bucheu*

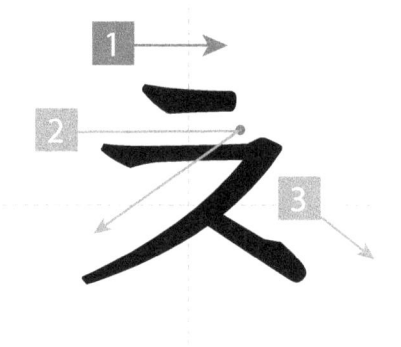

LEARN

Trace and draw this basic letter in the cells below.

PRACTICE

Now practice in these smaller cells.

EXAMPLE SYLLABLES

차	챠	처	쳐	초	쵸	추	츄	츠	치
cha	chya	cheo	chyeo	cho	chyo	chu	chyu	cheu	chi

ㅇ ㅇ n/a

NAME 이응 ieung

SAY
Initial - **silent**
Final - **ng** Pronounced like **the 'ng' in sang**

STYLES ㅇ ㅇ ㅇ ㅇ ㅇ ㅇ ㅇ

WRITE Made with a single, circular stroke.
The 'lump' is where a brush would first contact the paper.

IN USE 가방 bag   식당 restaurant, cafe
gabang   *sigdang*

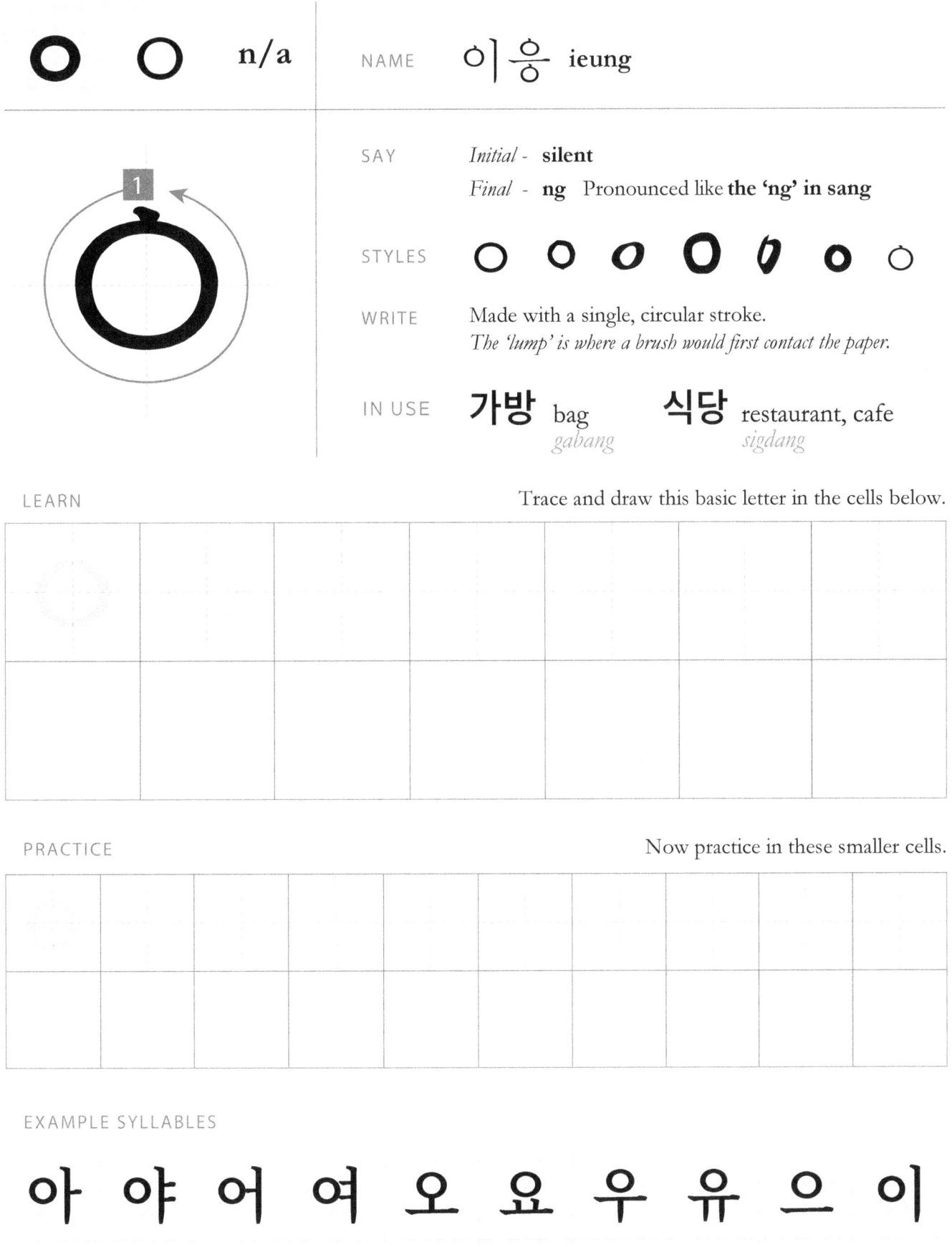

LEARN — Trace and draw this basic letter in the cells below.

PRACTICE — Now practice in these smaller cells.

EXAMPLE SYLLABLES

아 야 어 여 오 요 우 유 으 이
a ya eo yeo o yo u yu eu i

NAME	히읗 hieut
SAY	*Initial* - **h** Pronounced like **the 'h' in hot**
	Final - **t** Pronounced like **the 't' in hot**
STYLES	ㅎ ㅎ ㅎ ㅎ ㅎ ㅎ
WRITE	Drawn with three strokes.
IN USE	**한국** South Korea **학교** school
	Hanguk *haggyo*

LEARN

Trace and draw this basic letter in the cells below.

PRACTICE

Now practice in these smaller cells.

EXAMPLE SYLLABLES

하 야 허 혀 호 효 후 휴 흐 히

ha   hya   heo   hyeo   ho   hyo   hu   hyu   heu   hi

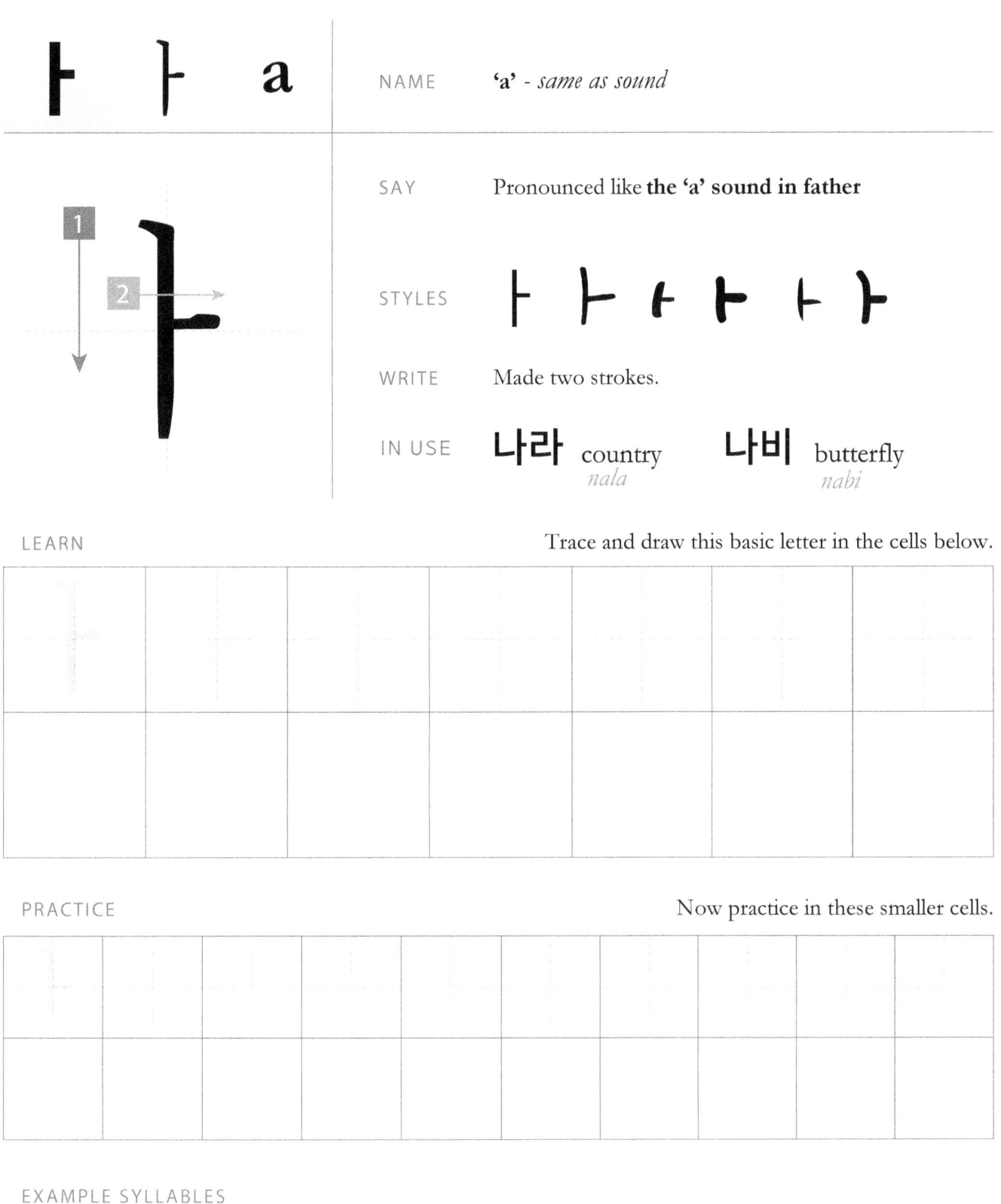

NAME	'a' - *same as sound*
SAY	Pronounced like **the 'a' sound in father**
STYLES	ㅏ ㅏ ㅏ ㅏ ㅏ
WRITE	Made two strokes.
IN USE	나라 country *nala* 나비 butterfly *nabi*

LEARN

Trace and draw this basic letter in the cells below.

PRACTICE

Now practice in these smaller cells.

EXAMPLE SYLLABLES

가 카 나 다 타 라 마 바 파 사 자 차 아 하
ga ka na da ta ra ma ba pa sa ja cha a ha

Hangul Vowels 31

ㅑ ya

NAME 'ya' - same as sound

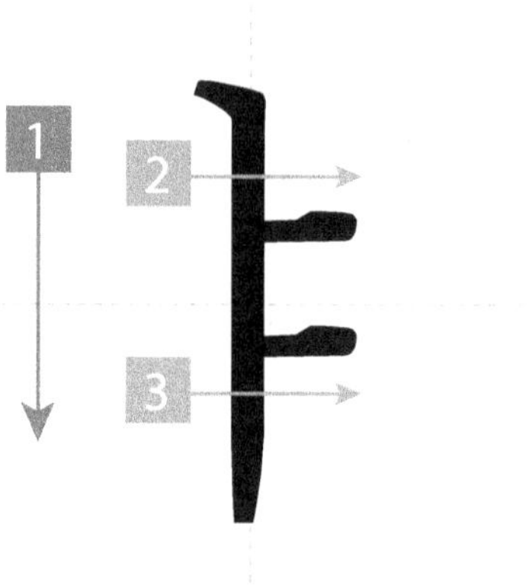

SAY Pronounced like **the 'ya' in yard**
Just as with 'a' but with a soft 'y' sound at the front.

STYLES ㅑ ㅑ ㅑ ㅑ ㅑ ㅑ

WRITE Made with three strokes.

IN USE 야구 baseball　　고양이 cat
yagu　　*goyangi*

LEARN　　Trace and draw this basic letter in the cells below.

PRACTICE　　Now practice in these smaller cells.

EXAMPLE SYLLABLES

갸	캬	냐	댜	탸	랴	먀	뱌	퍄	샤	쟈	챠	야	햐
gya	kya	nya	dya	tya	rya	mya	bya	pya	sya	jya	chya	ya	hya

NAME	'eo' - same as sound
SAY	Pronounced like **the 'u' sound in bus** *Mouth open in a long, tall shape, and keeping your lips still.*
STYLES	ㅓ ㅓ ㅓ ㅓ ㅓ
WRITE	Made with two strokes.
IN USE	단어 word *daneo* 영어 English (language) *yeongeo*

LEARN — Trace and draw this basic letter in the cells below.

PRACTICE — Now practice in these smaller cells.

EXAMPLE SYLLABLES

거 커 너 더 터 러 머 버 퍼 서 저 처 어 허

geo keo neo deo teo reo meo beo peo seo jeo cheo eo heo

ㅕ ㅕ yeo

NAME	**'yeo'** - *same as sound*
SAY	Pronounced like **the 'yu' in yum** *Just as with 'eo' but with a soft 'y' sound at the front.*
STYLES	ㅕ ㅕ ㅕ ㅕ ㅕ ㅕ
WRITE	Made with three strokes.
IN USE	**편지** letter **저녁** dinner, evening *pyeonji* *jeonyeog*

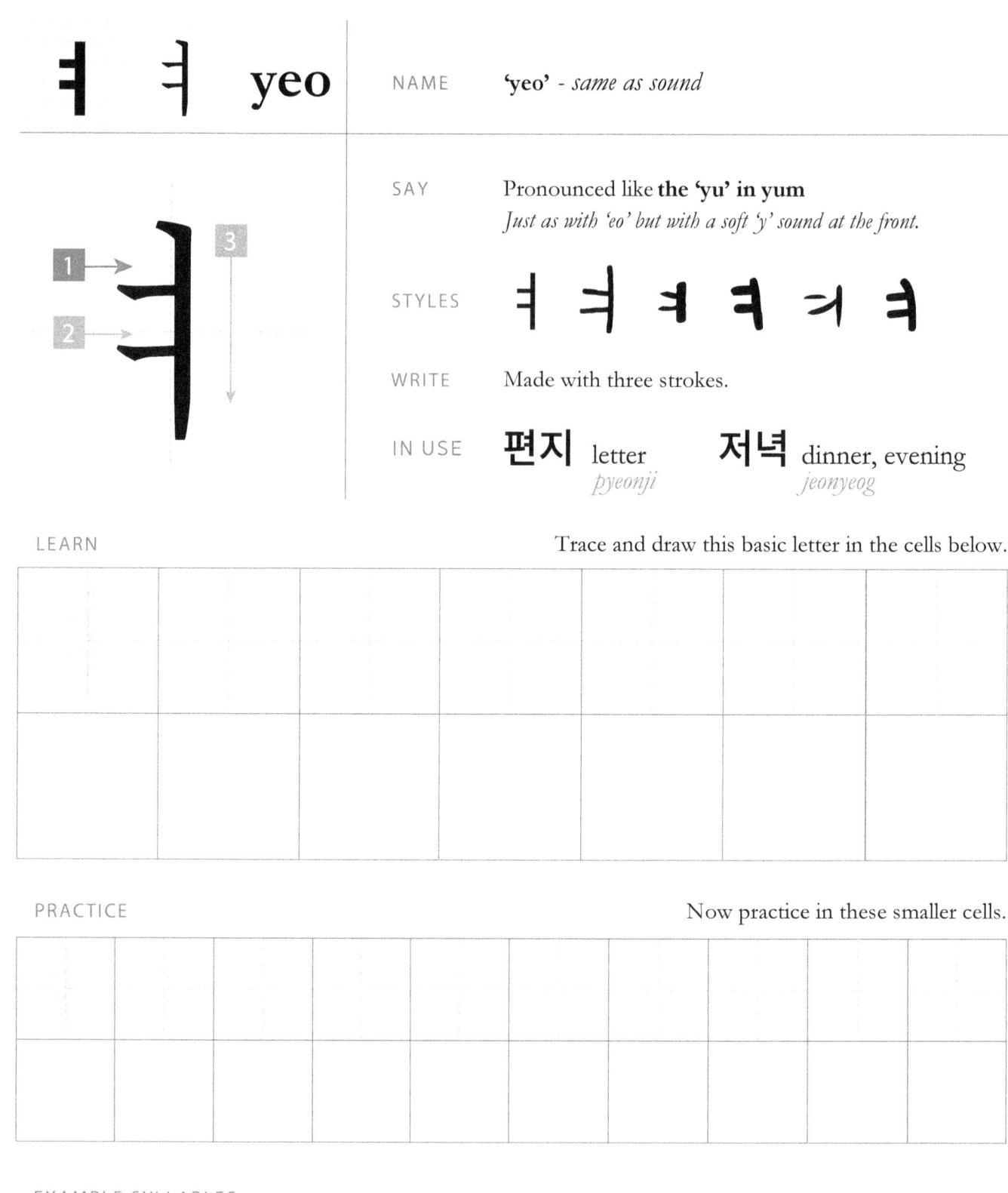

LEARN
Trace and draw this basic letter in the cells below.

PRACTICE
Now practice in these smaller cells.

EXAMPLE SYLLABLES

겨 켜 녀 뎌 텨 려 며 벼 펴 셔 져 쳐 여 혀

gyeo kyeo nyeo dyeo tyeo ryeo myeo byeo pyeo syeo jyeo chyeo yeo hyeo

ㅣ ㅣ i

NAME	'i' - same as sound
SAY	Pronounced like **the 'ee' in sleep or feet** *Wide mouth, teeth closer together (not closed)*
STYLES	ㅣ) ׀) ׀)
WRITE	Made with a single stroke.
IN USE	**아버지** father **어머니** mother **아니** no *abeoji* *eomeoni* *ani*

LEARN

Trace and draw this basic letter in the cells below.

PRACTICE

Now practice in these smaller cells.

EXAMPLE SYLLABLES

기 키 니 디 티 리 미 비 피 시 지 치 이 히

gi　ki　ni　di　ti　ri　mi　bi　pi　si　ji　chi　i　hi

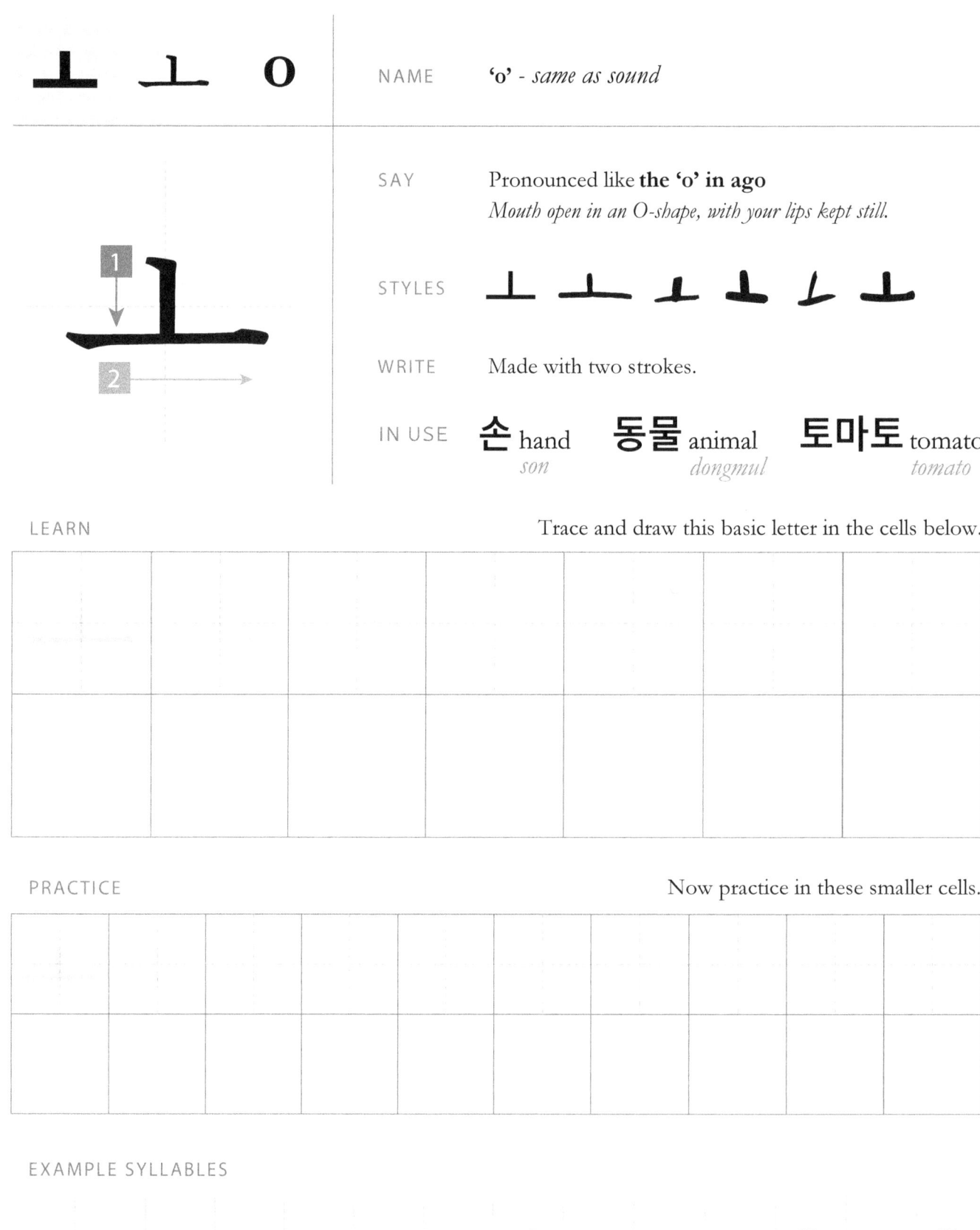

ㅛ ㅛ yo

NAME 'yo' - same as sound

SAY Sounds like **the 'yo' in yoga**
Just like letter 'o' but with a soft 'y' sound at the front.

STYLES ㅛ ㅛ ㅛ ㅛ ㅛ ㅛ

WRITE Drawn with three strokes.

IN USE 요요 yoyo   쉬워요 easy
yoyo   *swiwoyo*

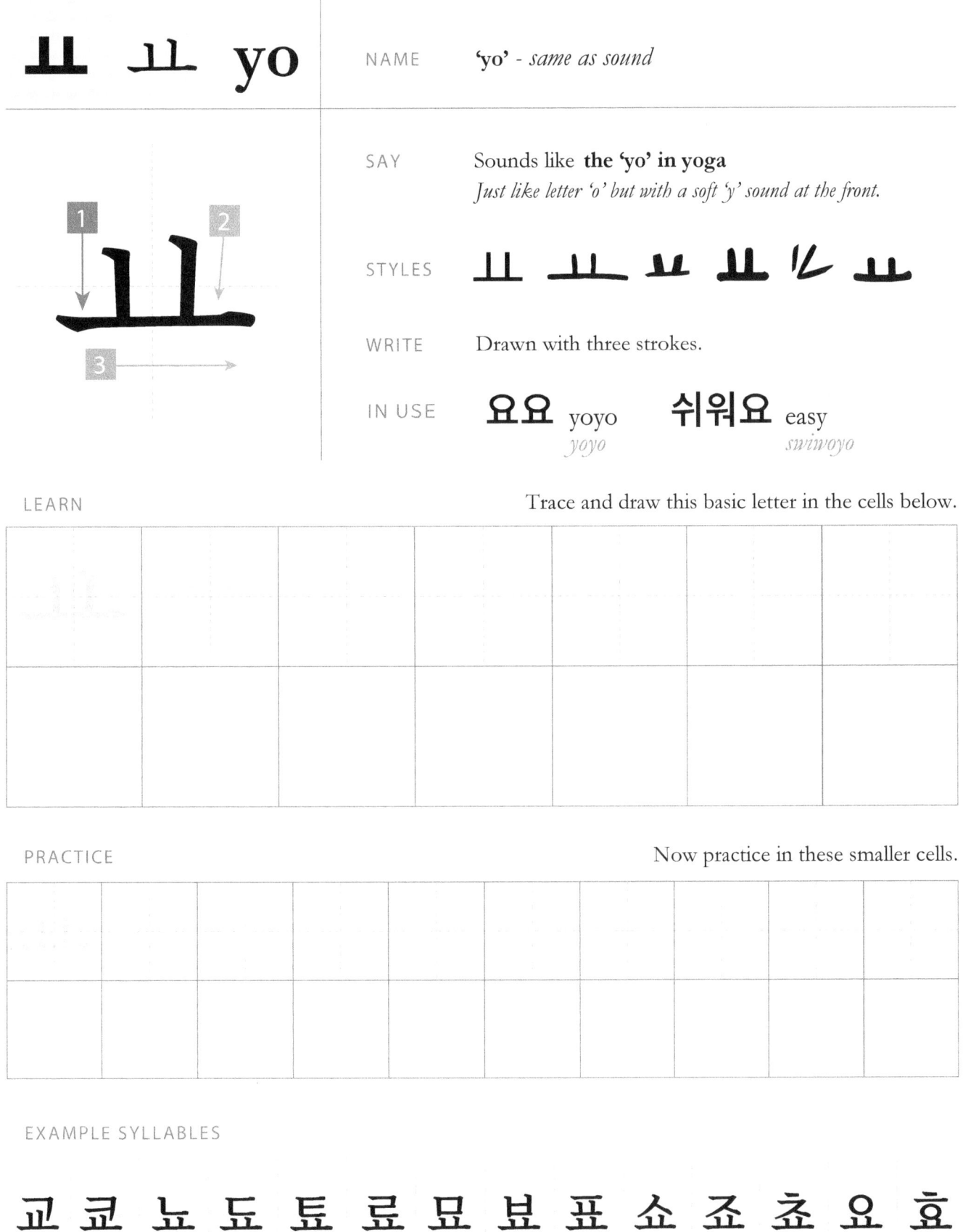

LEARN Trace and draw this basic letter in the cells below.

PRACTICE Now practice in these smaller cells.

EXAMPLE SYLLABLES

교	쿄	뇨	됴	툐	료	묘	뵤	표	쇼	죠	쵸	요	효
gyo	kyo	nyo	dyo	tyo	ryo	myo	byo	pyo	syo	jyo	chyo	yo	hyo

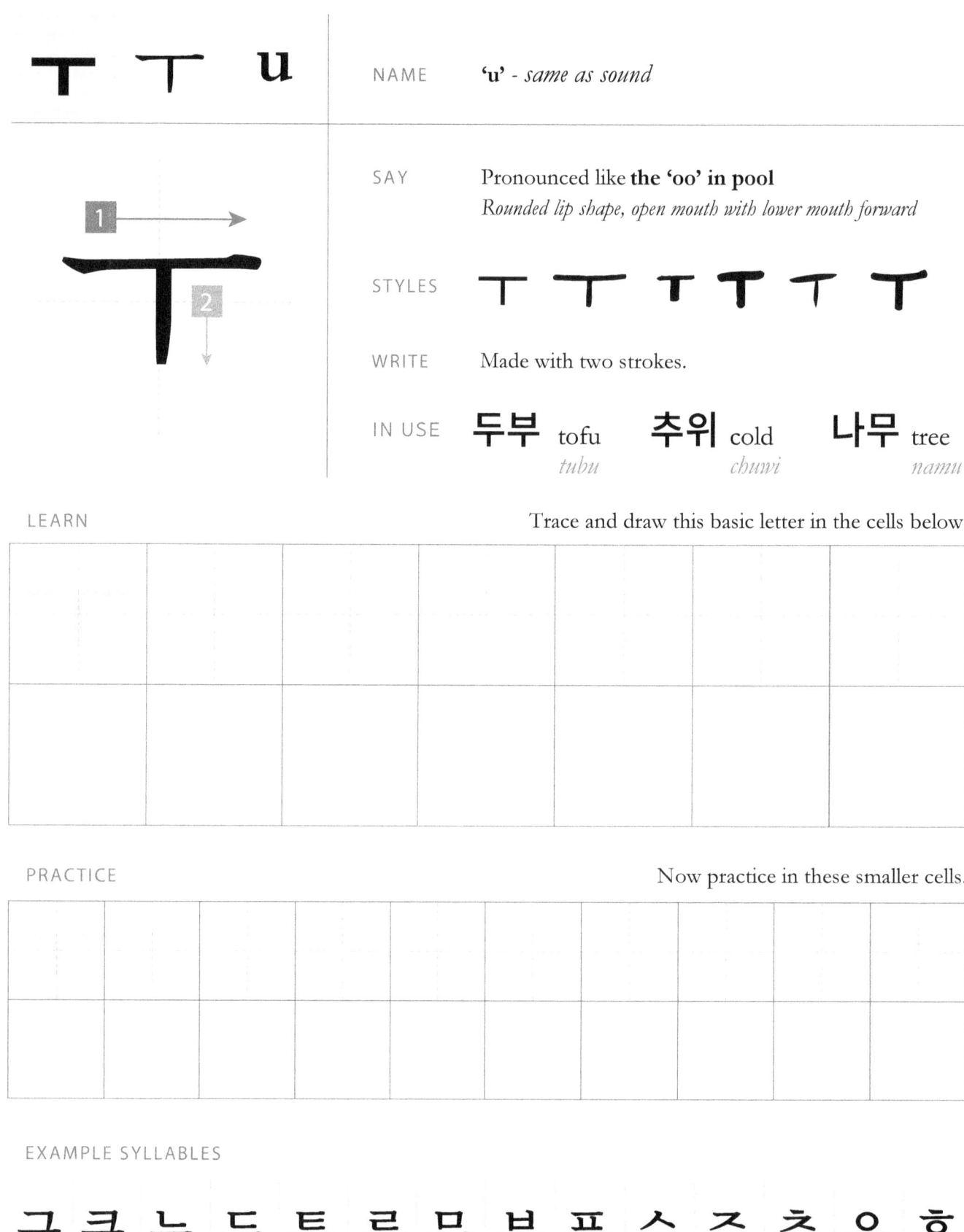

| ㅜ | ㅜ | u |

NAME   'u' - same as sound

SAY   Pronounced like **the 'oo' in pool**
Rounded lip shape, open mouth with lower mouth forward

STYLES   ㅜ ㅜ ㅜ ㅜ ㅜ ㅜ

WRITE   Made with two strokes.

IN USE   두부 tofu *tubu*   추위 cold *chuwi*   나무 tree *namu*

LEARN   Trace and draw this basic letter in the cells below.

PRACTICE   Now practice in these smaller cells.

EXAMPLE SYLLABLES

구	쿠	누	두	투	루	무	부	푸	수	주	추	우	후
gu	ku	nu	du	tu	ru	mu	bu	pu	su	ju	chu	u	hu

ㅠ ㅠ yu

NAME	'yu' - same as sound
SAY	Pronounced like **the word 'you'** *Just as with 'u' but with a soft 'y' sound at the front.*
STYLES	ㅠ ㅠ ㅠ ㅠ ㅠ ㅠ
WRITE	Drawn with three strokes.
IN USE	자유 freedom 컴퓨터 computer *chayu* *keompyuteo*

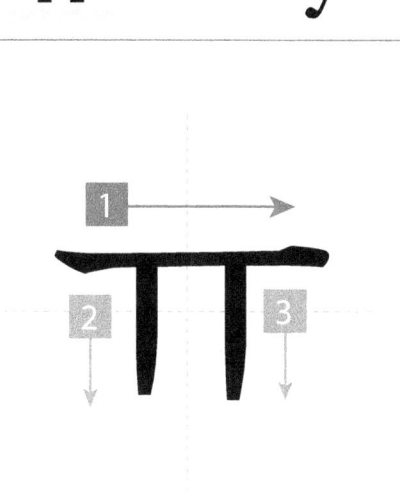

LEARN

Trace and draw this basic letter in the cells below.

PRACTICE

Now practice in these smaller cells.

EXAMPLE SYLLABLES

규 큐 뉴 듀 튜 류 뮤 뷰 퓨 슈 쥬 츄 유 휴

gyu kyu nyu dyu tyu ryu myu byu pyu syu jyu chyu yu hyu

— — eu

| NAME | 'eu' - *same as sound* |

SAY Sounds like **a disappointed 'eugh' noise**
*'Uh' with a wide mouth, corners pulled back,
teeth closer together (not closed)*

STYLES — — - — ‿ ⁀

WRITE Made with a single stroke.

IN USE 이름 name 퀴즈 quiz 카드 card
ileum *kwijeu* *kadeu*

LEARN — Trace and draw this basic letter in the cells below.

PRACTICE — Now practice in these smaller cells.

EXAMPLE SYLLABLES

그 크 느 드 트 르 므 브 프 스 즈 츠 으 흐

geu keu neu deu teu reu meu beu peu seu jeu cheu eu heu

Part 3

BASIC HANGUL REVISION & PRACTICE

DRILLS Combine these consonants with vowel 아 아 DESCRIBE THE SOUND

ㄱ							
ㅋ							
ㄴ							
ㄷ							
ㅌ							
ㄹ							

DRILLS Combine these consonants with vowel 야 야 DESCRIBE THE SOUND

ㅁ							
ㅂ							
ㅍ							
ㅅ							
ㅈ							
ㅊ							

NOTE: EXAMPLES ARE FOR WRITING PRACTICE AND MIGHT NOT BE COMMON.

DRILLS	Combine these consonants with vowel 어 **어**							DESCRIBE THE SOUND
ㄱ								
ㅋ								
ㄴ								
ㄷ								
ㅌ								
ㄹ								

DRILLS	Combine these consonants with vowel 여 **여**							DESCRIBE THE SOUND
ㅁ								
ㅂ								
ㅍ								
ㅅ								
ㅈ								
ㅊ								

(See Reference Charts - Page 123)

DRILLS	Combine these consonants with vowel 이 **이**							DESCRIBE THE SOUND
ㄱ								
ㅋ								
ㄴ								
ㄷ								
ㅌ								
ㄹ								

DRILLS	Combine these consonants with vowel 으 **으**							DESCRIBE THE SOUND
ㅁ								
ㅂ								
ㅍ								
ㅅ								
ㅈ								
ㅊ								

NOTE: EXAMPLES ARE FOR WRITING PRACTICE AND MIGHT NOT BE COMMON

DRILLS	Combine these consonants with vowel 오 오						DESCRIBE THE SOUND
ㄱ							
ㅋ							
ㄴ							
ㄷ							
ㅌ							
ㄹ							

DRILLS	Combine these consonants with vowel 요 요						DESCRIBE THE SOUND
ㅁ							
ㅂ							
ㅍ							
ㅅ							
ㅈ							
ㅊ							

(See Reference Charts - Page 123)

DRILLS	Combine these consonants with vowel 우 우								DESCRIBE THE SOUND
ㄱ									
ㅋ									
ㄴ									
ㄷ									
ㅌ									
ㄹ									

DRILLS	Combine these consonants with vowel 유 유								DESCRIBE THE SOUND
ㅁ									
ㅂ									
ㅍ									
ㅅ									
ㅈ									
ㅊ									

NOTE: EXAMPLES ARE FOR WRITING PRACTICE AND MIGHT NOT BE COMMON

DRILLS	Combine these consonants with vowel 오 오									DESCRIBE THE SOUND
ㄱ										
ㅋ										
ㄴ										
ㄷ										
ㅌ										
ㄹ										

DRILLS	Combine these consonants with vowel 요 요									DESCRIBE THE SOUND
ㅁ										
ㅂ										
ㅍ										
ㅅ										
ㅈ										
ㅊ										

(See Reference Charts - Page 123)

QUICK QUIZ! A

Let's put your memory to the test!

1 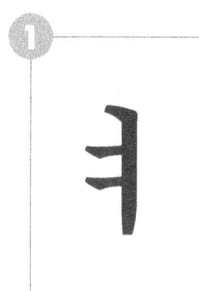 This letter sounds like ____ ?
- A. the **'yu'** in yum
- B. the **'o'** sound in orange
- C. the **'ee'** in sleep
- D. the **'ya'** in yard

2 ____ is pronounced like the **'p'** in pizza?
- A. ㅠ B. ㅍ
- C. ㅛ D. ㅂ

3 Which of these consonants do we use as a silent placeholder with every vowel?

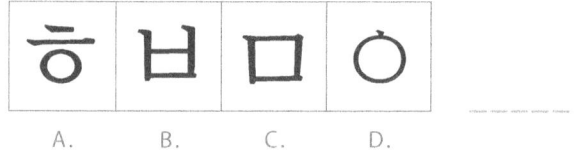

A.   B.   C.   D.

4 ____ is pronounced like the **'j'** in juice?
- A. ㅅ B. ㅊ
- C. ㅈ D. ㅎ

5 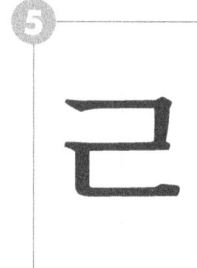 How many strokes does it take to draw this character?
Can you draw the order on the image?
- A. 2 B. 4
- C. 3 D. 5

6  How many strokes does it take to draw this character?
Can you draw the order on the image?
- A. 2 B. 4
- C. 3 D. 5

7 ____ is pronounced like the **'ee'** in sleep?
- A. ㅜ B. ㅡ
- C. ㅣ D. ㅗ

8 Which of these syllable blocks are wrong?

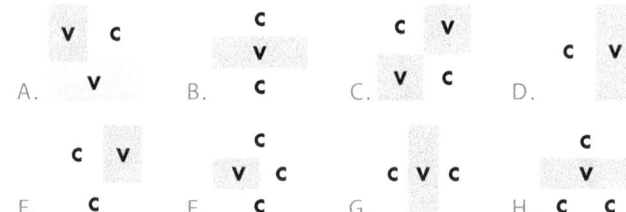

A.   B.   C.   D.

E.   F.   G.   H.

9 ____ is pronounced like the **'d'** in door?
- A. ㅋ B. ㄷ
- C. ㄴ D. ㅌ

10  This letter sounds like ____ ?
- A. the **'k'** in 'kite'
- B. the **'ch'** in chat
- C. the **'c'** in cake
- D. the **'g'** in gum

(See Answers - Page 128)

Part 4

COMPOUND HANGUL LETTERS

COMBINATION LETTERS

There are an additional 16 letters to learn after the basic Hangul and they are often called *compound letters* - but they are not as complicated as they sound. In fact, they are simply made with combinations of the letters that you can now read and write already!

DOUBLE CONSONANTS

This set of letters is relatively small - there are just **5 'tensed' double consonants** to learn and they are simply two of the same letters together! Each of them can be used in as initial consonants but only ㄲ and ㅆ can be **batchim** *(we will look at this later)*.

Pronunciation is like the single-letter versions, except you tense your mouth when you say them - *hence the name!*

By taking a momentary pause as you are about to pronounce a letter, you naturally build up that little bit of extra force behind the letter that follows. Here is a quick exercise to help you understand the **'tensed'** sounds better:

Say the word 'top' and then afterwards say the word 'stop'. Repeat and pay special attention to the '-t' sounds. Can you feel and hear a difference between the two?

When paired this way, the double consonants count as a single letter when we write them. As such, the space they occupy in a syllable is the same as any other individual letter. Let us now check how double consonants look inside the syllable layouts below:

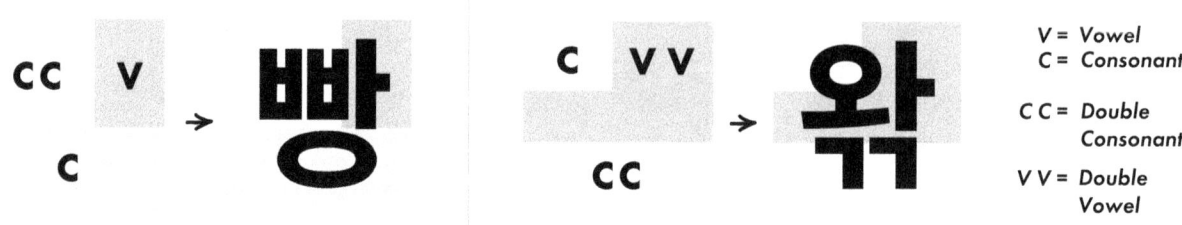

Additional Letters

DOUBLE VOWELS

These compound vowels, or **diphthongs**, are made from two basic vowels. The sounds that individual letters represent are joined together to make a new sound - we pronounce the diphthongs by saying the two joined up vowels quite quickly, as one smooth sound:

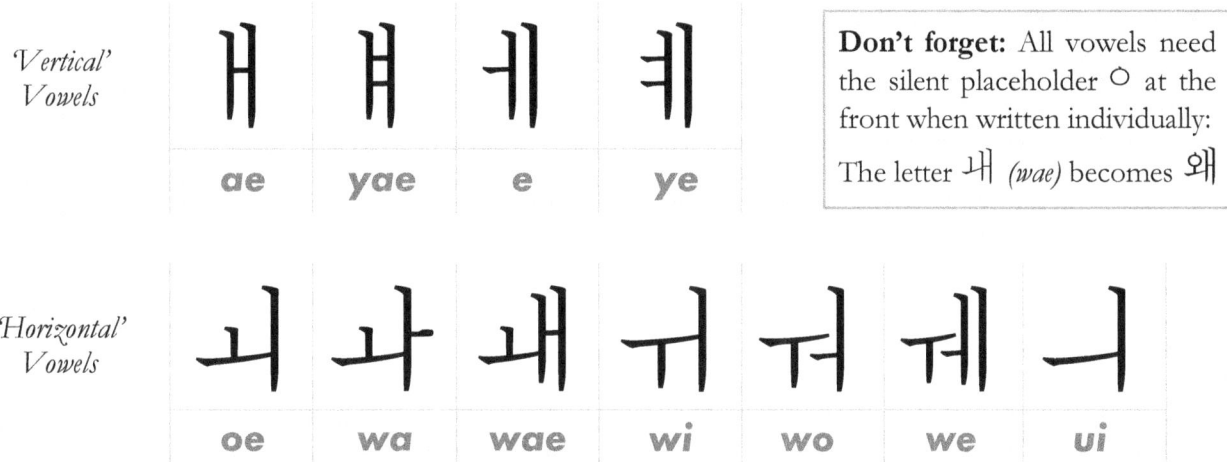

Syllable blocks with diphthongs also have varying layouts depending on the shapes of the vowels inside them and the number of letters they contain:

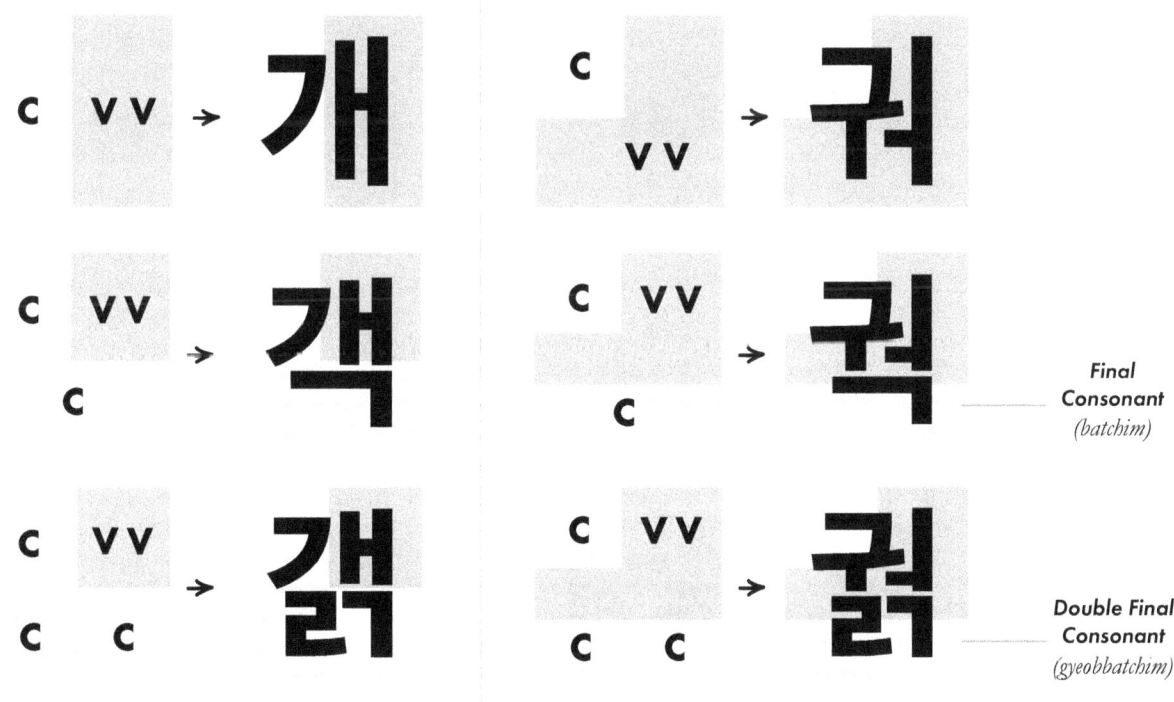

Compound Hangul

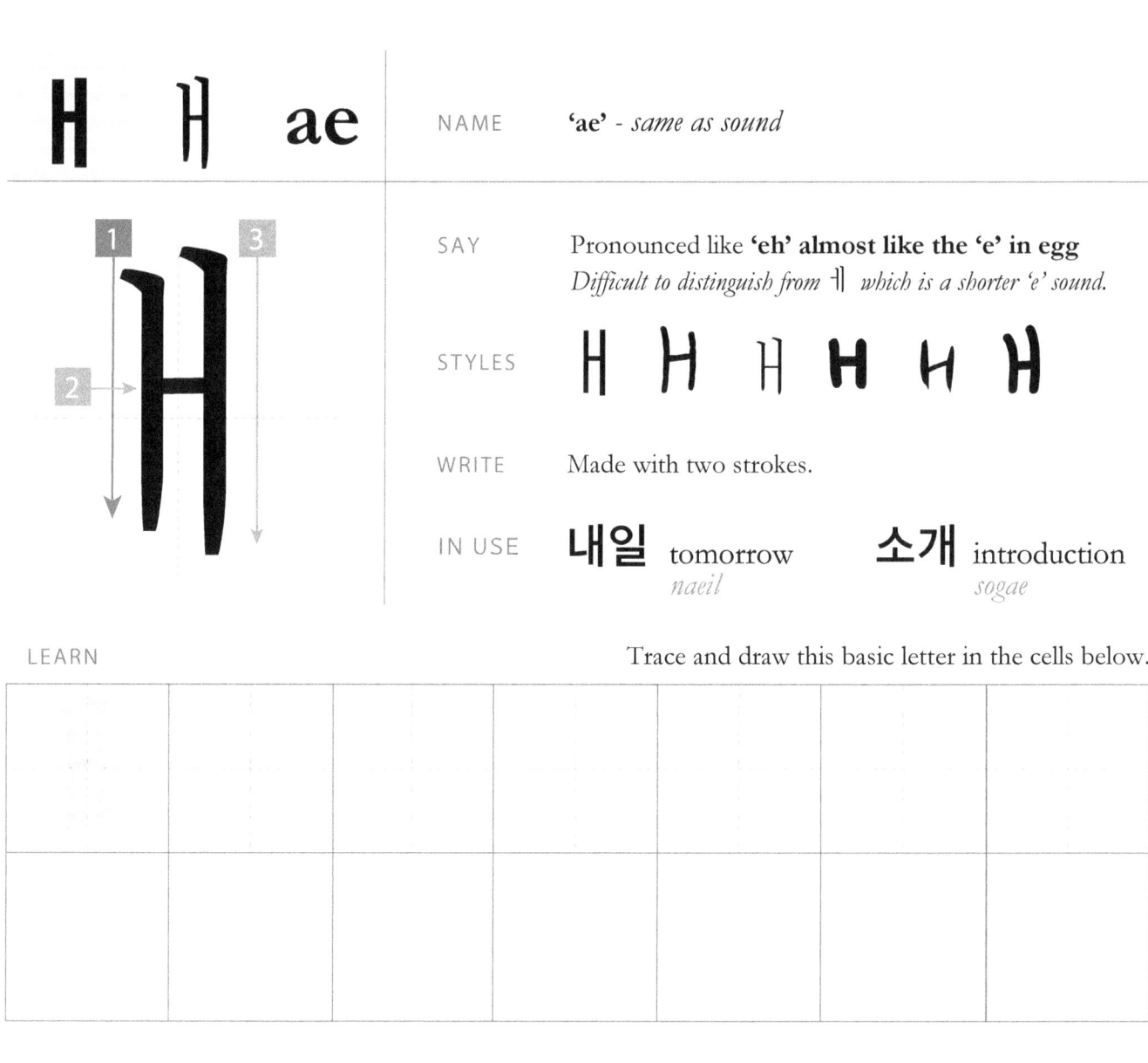

NAME	'ae' - *same as sound*	
SAY	Pronounced like **'eh' almost like the 'e' in egg** *Difficult to distinguish from* ㅔ *which is a shorter 'e' sound.*	
STYLES	ㅐ ㅐ ㅐ ㅐ ㅐ ㅐ	
WRITE	Made with two strokes.	
IN USE	**내일** tomorrow *naeil*	**소개** introduction *sogae*

LEARN — Trace and draw this basic letter in the cells below.

PRACTICE — Now practice in these smaller cells.

EXAMPLE SYLLABLES

개	캐	내	대	태	래	매	배	패	새	재	채	애	해
gae	kae	nae	dae	tae	rae	mae	bae	pae	sae	jae	chae	ae	hae

ㅐ ㅒ yae

NAME 'yae' - same as sound

SAY Pronounced like **'yeh' similar to 'yeah'**
Just like 'ae' with a 'y' sound at the front.

STYLES ㅒ ㅒ ㅒ ㅒ ㅒ ㅒ

WRITE Made with four strokes.

IN USE 얘기 story
yaegi

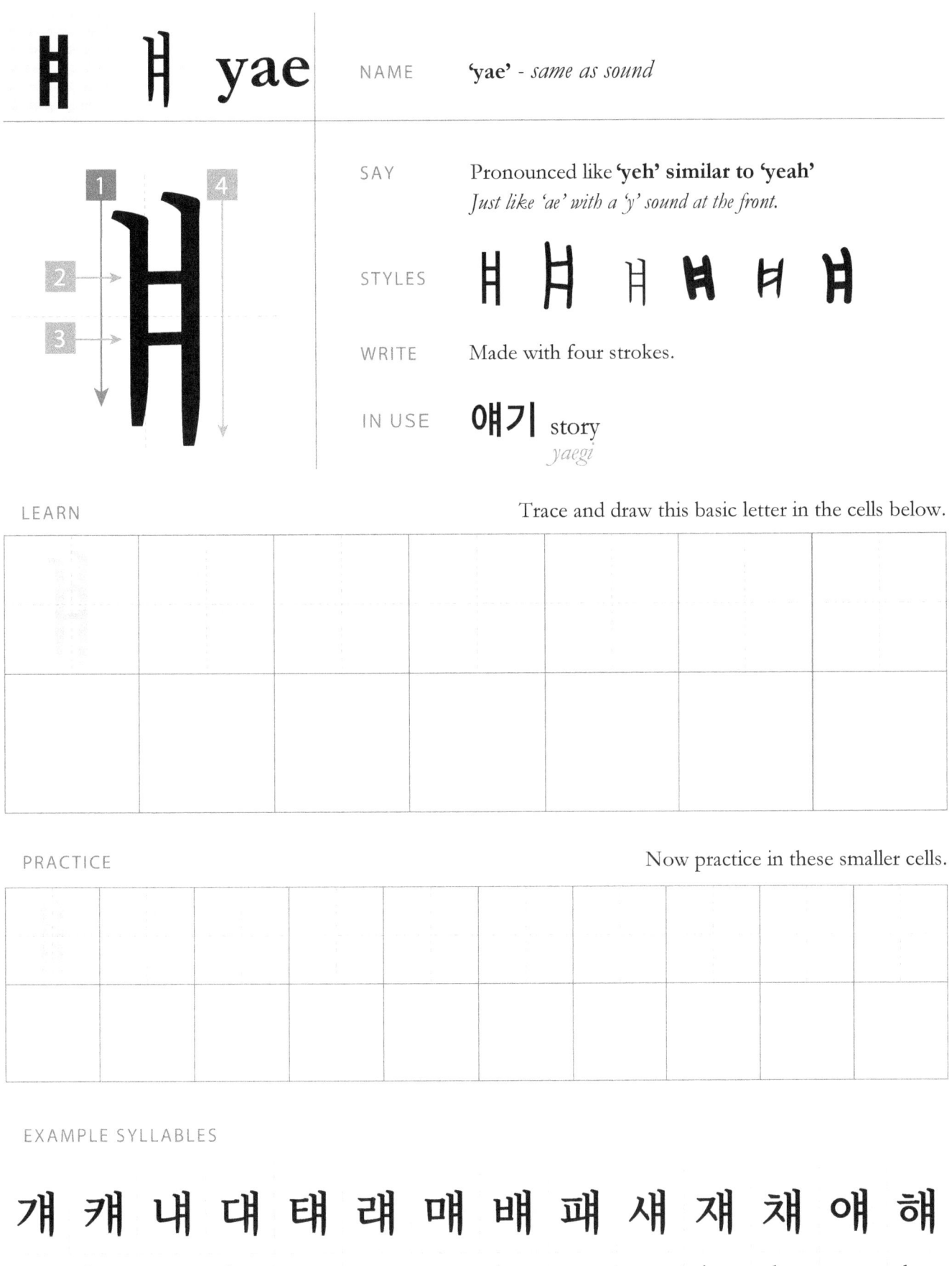

LEARN — Trace and draw this basic letter in the cells below.

PRACTICE — Now practice in these smaller cells.

EXAMPLE SYLLABLES

걔	걔	냬	댸	턔	럐	먜	뱨	퍠	섀	쟤	챼	얘	햬
gyae	kyae	nyae	dyae	tyae	ryae	myae	byae	pyae	syae	jyae	chyae	yae	hyae

Compound Vowels

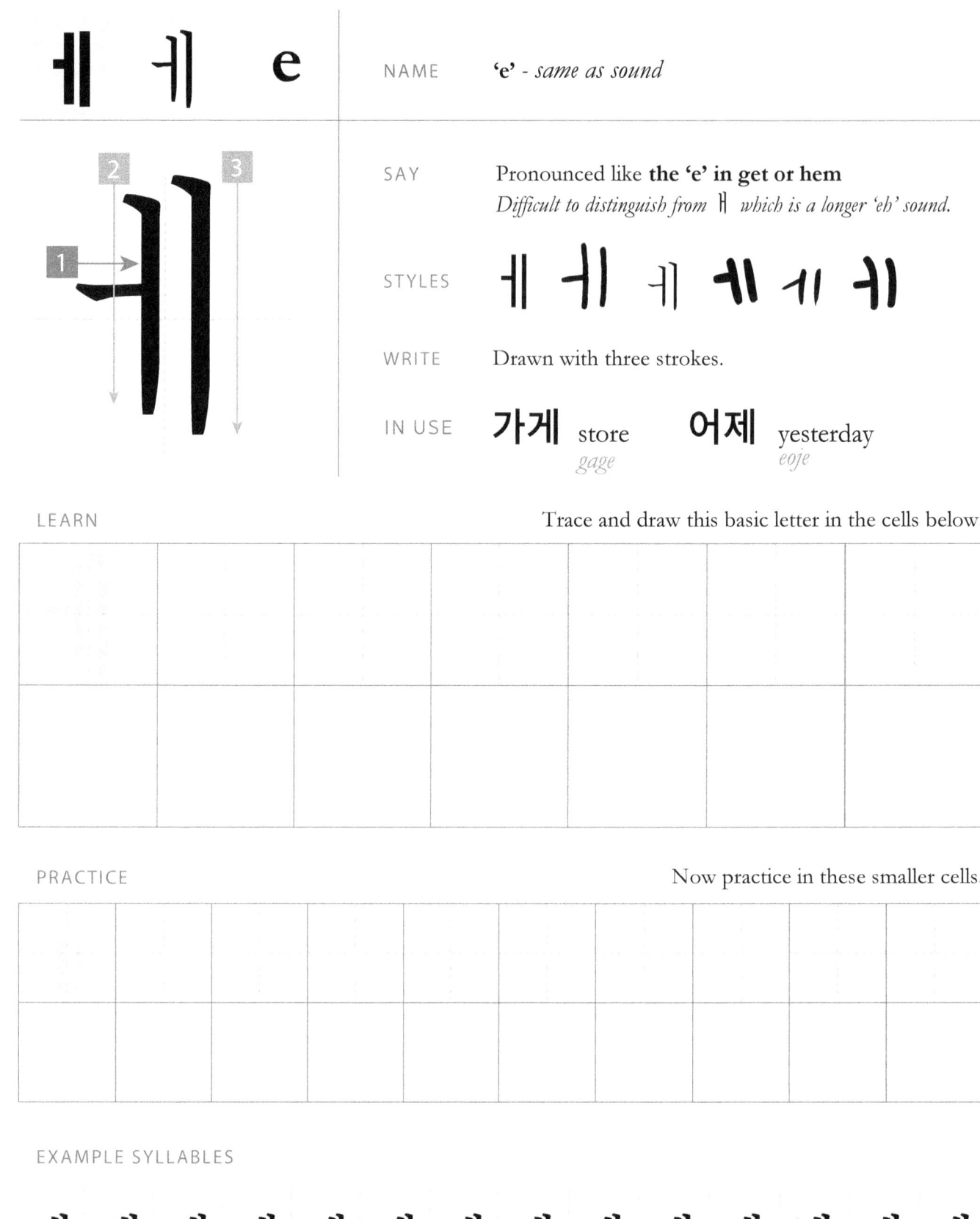

NAME	'e' - *same as sound*
SAY	Pronounced like **the 'e' in get or hem** *Difficult to distinguish from* ㅐ *which is a longer 'eh' sound.*
STYLES	ㅔ ㅔ ㅔ ㅔ ㅔ
WRITE	Drawn with three strokes.
IN USE	가게 store *gage* 어제 yesterday *eoje*

LEARN — Trace and draw this basic letter in the cells below.

PRACTICE — Now practice in these smaller cells.

EXAMPLE SYLLABLES

게 케 네 데 테 레 메 베 페 세 제 체 에 헤
ge ke ne de te re me be pe se je coe e he

ㅖ ㅖ ye

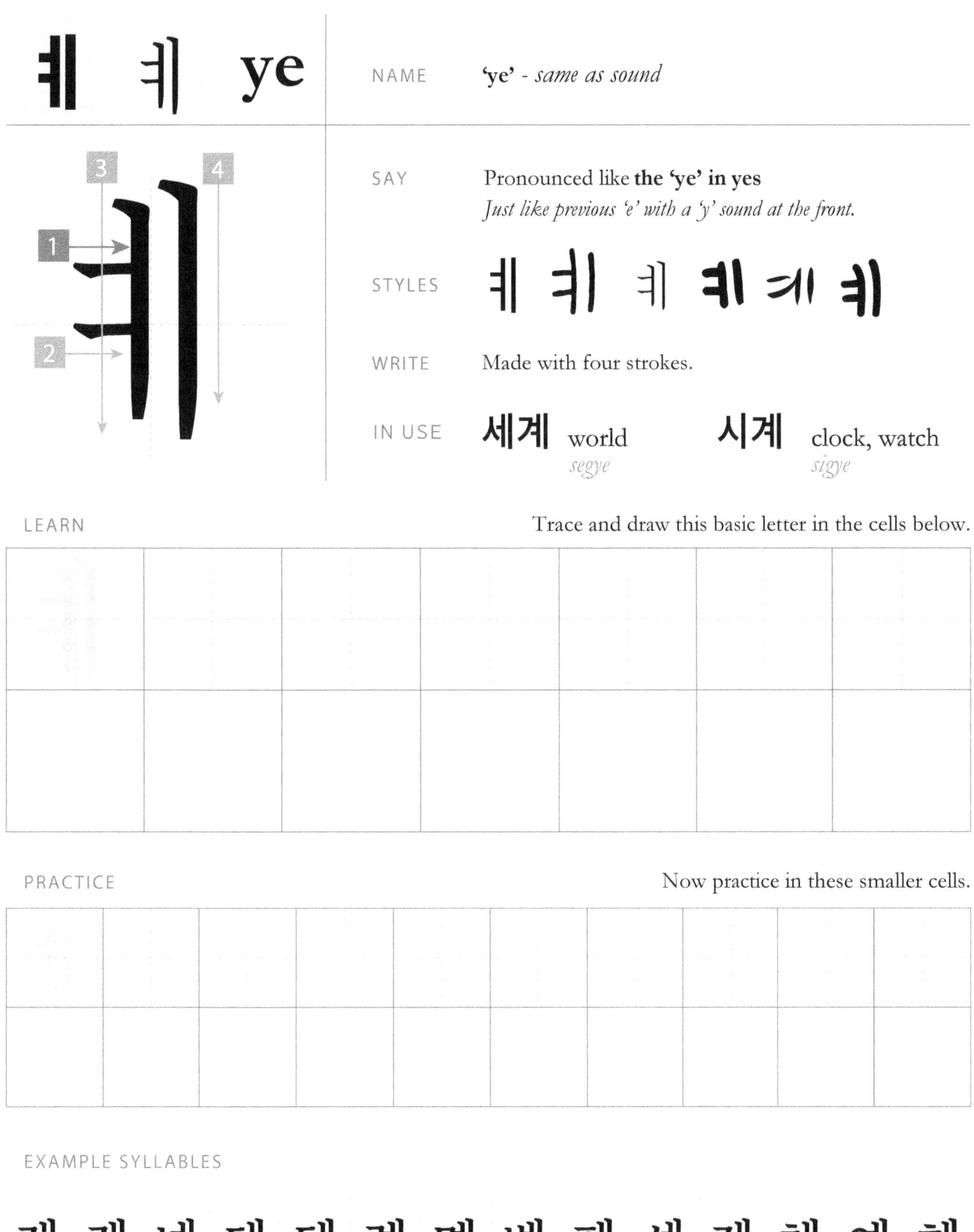

NAME	'ye' - *same as sound*
SAY	Pronounced like **the 'ye' in yes** *Just like previous 'e' with a 'y' sound at the front.*
STYLES	ㅖ ㅖ ㅖ ㅖ ㅖ ㅖ
WRITE	Made with four strokes.
IN USE	세계 world *segye* 　　시계 clock, watch *sigye*

LEARN — Trace and draw this basic letter in the cells below.

PRACTICE — Now practice in these smaller cells.

EXAMPLE SYLLABLES

계 켸 녜 뎨 톄 례 몌 볘 폐 셰 졔 쳬 예 혜

gye kye nye dye tye rye mye bye pye sye jye chye ye hye

ㅚ ㅚ oe

NAME	'oe' - *same as sound*
SAY	Pronounced as **'weh', just like the 'we' in wet** *Like 'oh-eh' but as a single smooth sound*
STYLES	ㅚ ㅚ ㅚ ㅚ ㅚ ㅚ
WRITE	Drawn with three strokes.
IN USE	**뇌** brain *noe* **회사** company *hoesa*

LEARN

Trace and draw this basic letter in the cells below.

PRACTICE

Now practice in these smaller cells.

EXAMPLE SYLLABLES

괴 쾨 뇌 되 퇴 뢰 뫼 뵈 푀 쇠 죄 최 외 회

goe koe noe doe toe roe moe boe poe soe joe choe oe hoe

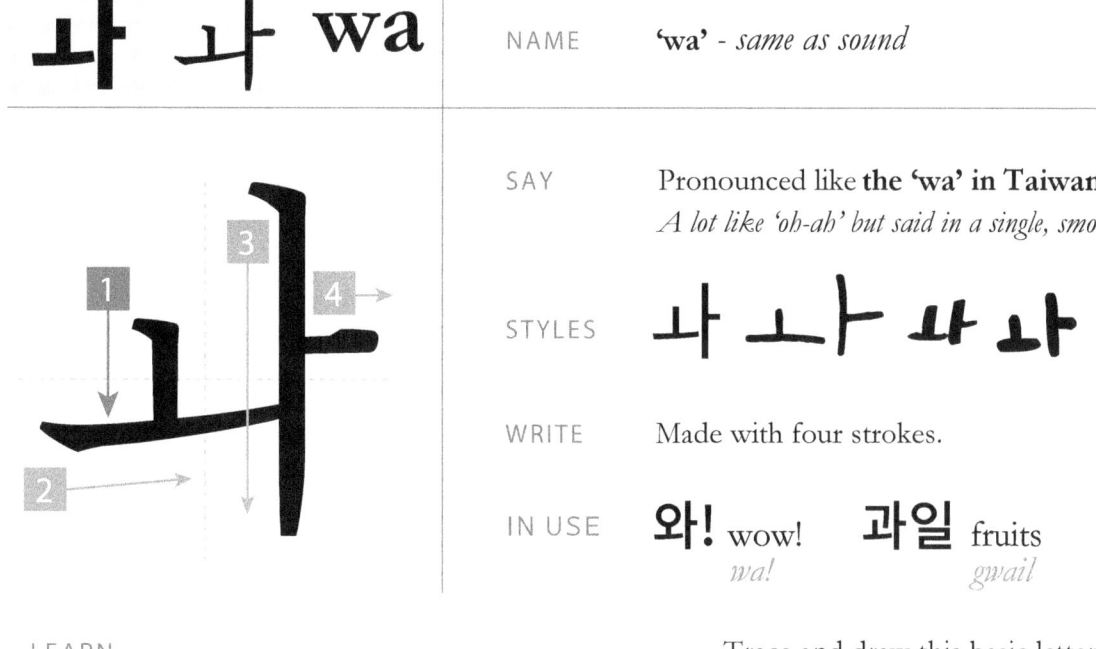

NAME	'wa' - same as sound
SAY	Pronounced like **the 'wa' in Taiwan, with a soft 'w'**. *A lot like 'oh-ah' but said in a single, smooth sound.*
STYLES	과 과 과 과 과 과
WRITE	Made with four strokes.
IN USE	와! wow! *wa!* 과일 fruits *gwail* 사과 apple *sagwa*

LEARN

Trace and draw this basic letter in the cells below.

PRACTICE

Now practice in these smaller cells.

EXAMPLE SYLLABLES

과 콰 놔 돠 톼 롸 뫄 봐 퐈 솨 좌 촤 와 화

gwa kwa nwa dwa twa rwa mwa bwa pwa swa jwa chwa wa hwa

내 내 wae

NAME — 'wae' - same as sound

SAY — Pronounced like **the 'we' in west, with a soft 'w'**
Essentially 'oh-ae' but said in a single, smooth sound.

STYLES — 내 내 내 내 내 내

WRITE — Drawn with five strokes.

IN USE — **왜요?** why? *waeyo?*   **인쇄** print *inswae*   **돼지** pig *dwaeji*

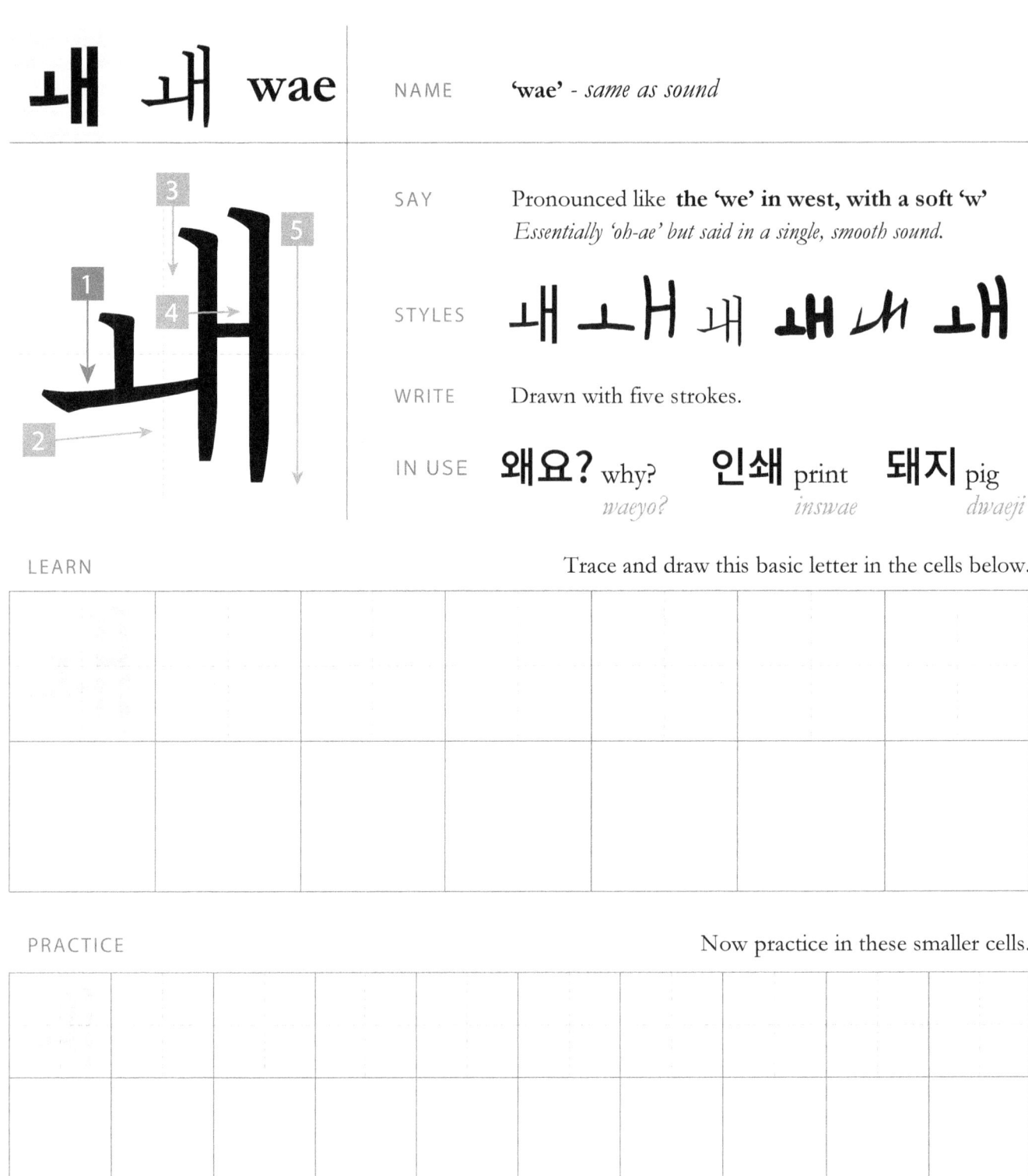

LEARN — Trace and draw this basic letter in the cells below.

PRACTICE — Now practice in these smaller cells.

EXAMPLE SYLLABLES

괘	쾌	내	돼	퇘	뢔	뫠	봬	퐤	쇄	좨	쵀	왜	홰
gwae	kwae	nwae	dwae	twae	rwae	mwae	bwae	pwae	swae	jwae	chwae	wae	hwae

ㅟ ㅟ wi

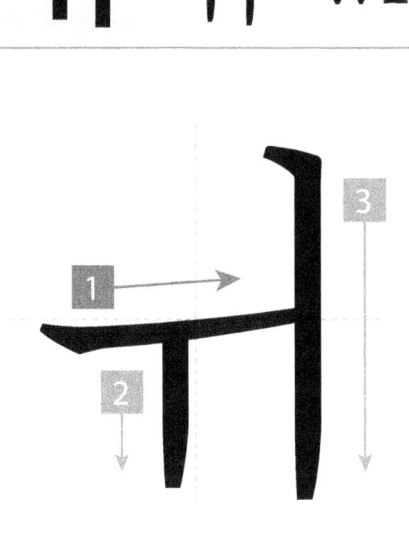

NAME	**'wi'** - *same as sound*
SAY	Pronounced like **the 'we' in week, with a soft 'w'** *Sounds like 'oo-ee' but said in a single, smooth sound.*
STYLES	ㅟ ㅟ ㅟ ㅟ ㅟ ㅟ
WRITE	Made with three strokes.
IN USE	**키위** kiwi *kiwi* **바퀴** wheel *bakwi* **귀걸이** earrings *gwigeoli*

LEARN   Trace and draw this basic letter in the cells below.

PRACTICE   Now practice in these smaller cells.

EXAMPLE SYLLABLES

귀	퀴	뉘	뒤	튀	뤼	뮈	뷔	퓌	쉬	쥐	취	위	휘
gwi	kwi	nwi	dwi	twi	rwi	mwi	bwi	pwi	swi	jwi	chwi	wi	hwi

ㅝ ㅝ wo

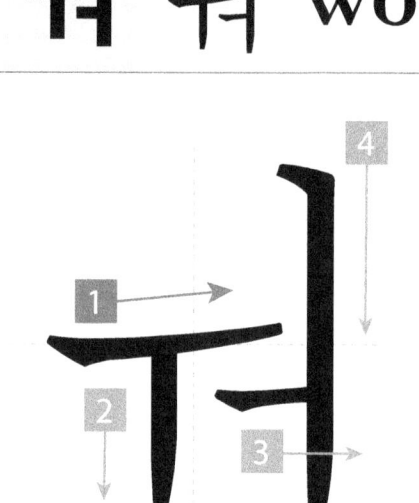

NAME	'wo' - same as sound
SAY	Pronounced like **the 'wo' in wok, with a soft 'w'** *Sounds like 'uh-or' said in short, smooth way.*
STYLES	ㅝ ㅝ ㅝ ㅝ ㅝ ㅝ
WRITE	Drawn with four strokes.
IN USE	소원 wish *sowon* 법원 courthouse *beob-won*

LEARN   Trace and draw this basic letter in the cells below.

PRACTICE   Now practice in these smaller cells.

EXAMPLE SYLLABLES

궈	쿼	눠	둬	퉈	뤄	뭐	붜	풔	숴	줘	춰	워	훠
gwo	kwo	nwo	dwo	two	rwo	mwo	bwo	pwo	swo	jwo	chwo	wo	hwo

ㅞ ㅞ we

NAME	'we' - same as sound
SAY	Pronounced like **'we'** in west or wet, with a soft 'w' *Sounds like 'o-eh' and hard to distinguish from 외 (oe)*
STYLES	ㅞ ㅞ ㅞ ㅞ ㅞ ㅞ
WRITE	Drawn with five strokes.
IN USE	웨딩 wedding *weding* (features in very few words)

LEARN

Trace and draw this basic letter in the cells below.

PRACTICE

Now practice in these smaller cells.

EXAMPLE SYLLABLES

궤	퀘	눼	뒈	퉤	뤠	뭬	붸	풰	쉐	줴	췌	웨	훼
gwe	kwe	nwe	dwe	twe	rwe	mwe	bwe	pwe	swe	jwe	chwe	we	hwe

61

ㅢ ui

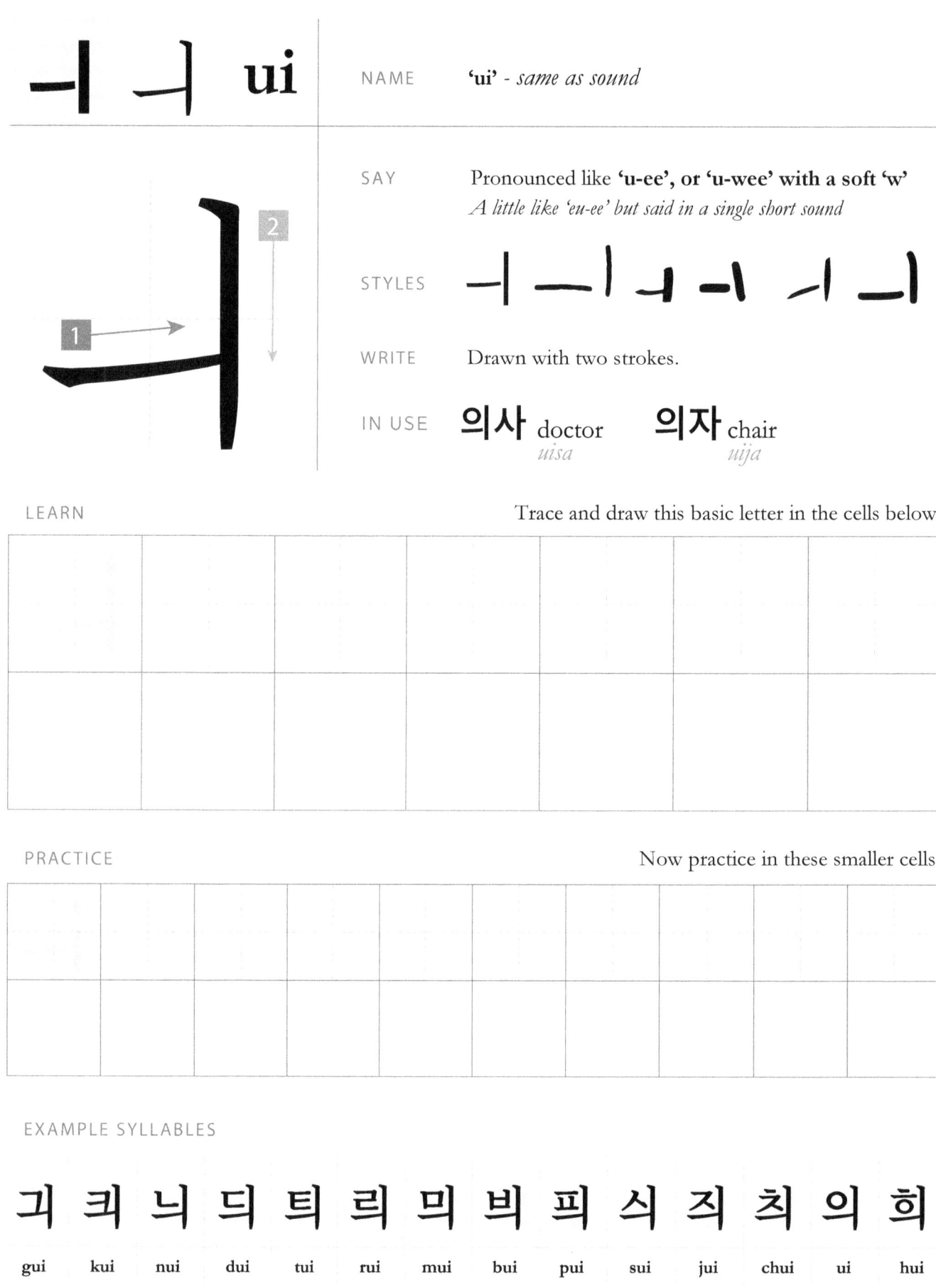

NAME 'ui' - same as sound

SAY Pronounced like **'u-ee'**, **or 'u-wee' with a soft 'w'**
A little like 'eu-ee' but said in a single short sound

STYLES ㅢ ㅢ ㅢ ㅢ ㅢ ㅢ

WRITE Drawn with two strokes.

IN USE 의사 doctor 의자 chair
uisa *uija*

LEARN   Trace and draw this basic letter in the cells below.

PRACTICE   Now practice in these smaller cells.

EXAMPLE SYLLABLES

긔 킈 늬 듸 틔 릐 믜 븨 픠 싀 즤 츼 의 희

gui kui nui dui tui rui mui bui pui sui jui chui ui hui

ㄲ ㄲ gg

NAME 쌍기역 ssang giyeok

SAY Pronounced like **'guh'**, similar to the **'g'** in great
Sounds similar to ㄱ (giyeok), but more forced and tense.

STYLES ㄲ ㄲ ㄲ ㄲ ㄲ ㄲ

WRITE Draw giyeok twice, with two strokes in total.

IN USE 낚시 fishing *naggsi*   토끼 rabbit *toggi*

LEARN — Trace and draw this basic letter in the cells below.

PRACTICE — Now practice in these smaller cells.

EXAMPLE SYLLABLES

까 꺄 꺼 껴 꼬 꾜 꾸 뀨 끄 끼
gga ggya ggeo ggyeo ggo ggyo ggu ggyu ggeu ggi

Double Consonants

ㄸ ㄸ dd

NAME 쌍디귿 ssang digeut

SAY Pronounced like **the 'd' sound in department**
Sounds similar to ㄷ (digeut), but more forced and tense.

STYLES ㄸ ㄸ ㄸ ㄸ ㄸ ㄸ

WRITE Made with four strokes, drawing digeut twice.

IN USE 머리띠 head band   뜨거운 hot
meoliddi   *ddeugeoun*

LEARN
Trace and draw this basic letter in the cells below.

PRACTICE
Now practice in these smaller cells.

EXAMPLE SYLLABLES

따 땨 떠 뗘 또 뚀 뚜 뜌 뜨 띠

dda ddya ddeo ddyeo ddo ddyo ddu ddyu ddeu ddi

ㅃ ㅃ bb

NAME	쌍 비읍 **ssang bieup**
SAY	Pronounced like **the 'b' in boy or banana**. *Sounds similar to ㅂ (bieup), but more forced and tense.*
STYLES	ㅃ ㅃ ㅃ ㅃ ㅃ ㅃ
WRITE	Draw bieup twice, with eight strokes in total.
IN USE	빵 bread *bbang* 빠른 fast *bbaleun* 바쁜 busy *babbeun*

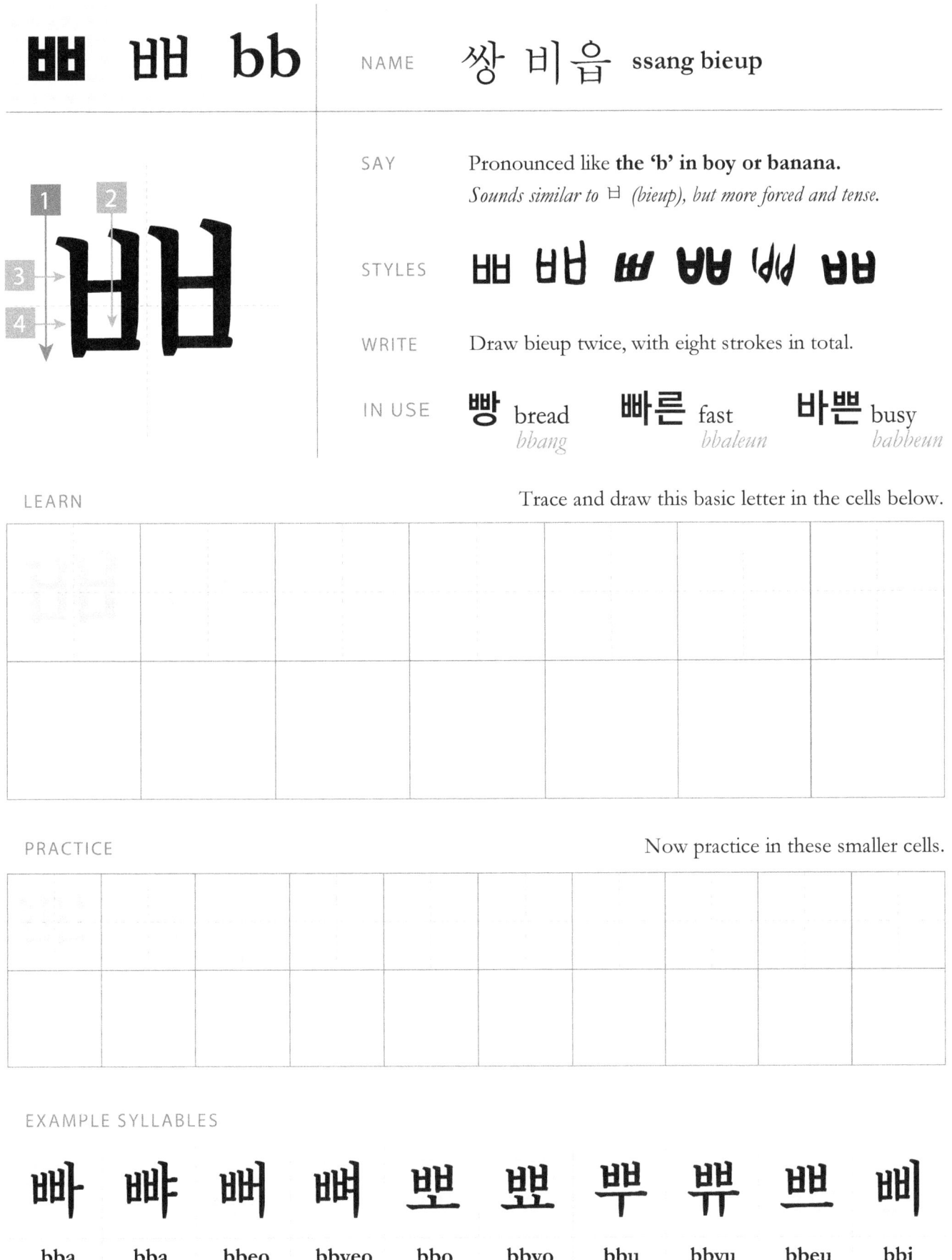

LEARN
Trace and draw this basic letter in the cells below.

PRACTICE
Now practice in these smaller cells.

EXAMPLE SYLLABLES

빠	빠	뻐	뼈	뽀	뾰	뿌	쀼	쁘	삐
bba	bba	bbeo	bbyeo	bbo	bbyo	bbu	bbyu	bbeu	bbi

ㅆ 从 ss

NAME 쌍시옷 ssang siot

SAY Pronounced as **a 's-' sound, with force at the beginning.** *Sounds similar to ㅅ (siot), but tensed.*

STYLES ㅆ ㅆ ㅆ ㅆ ㅆ ㅆ

WRITE Write siot twice, with four strokes in total.

IN USE 비싼 expensive *bissan*   싼 cheap *ssan*

LEARN

Trace and draw this basic letter in the cells below.

PRACTICE

Now practice in these smaller cells.

EXAMPLE SYLLABLES

싸	쌰	써	쎠	쏘	쑈	쑤	쓔	쓰	씨
ssa	ssya	sseo	ssyeo	sso	ssyo	ssu	ssyu	sseu	ssi

ㅉ ㅉ jj

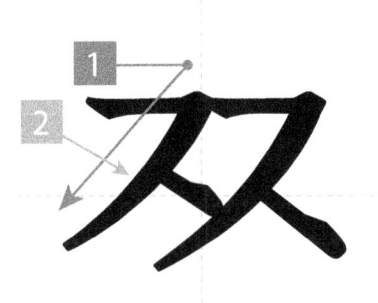

NAME	쌍지읒 **ssang jieut**
SAY	Pronounced like **the 'j' in job, with force at the start** *Sounds similar to ㅈ (jieut), but more tense.*
STYLES	ㅉ ㅉ **ㅉ** ㅉ ㅉ ㅉ
WRITE	Draw jieut twice, using four strokes in total.
IN USE	**찌개** stew or soup **짜다** salty *jjigae* *jjada*

LEARN   Trace and draw this basic letter in the cells below.

PRACTICE   Now practice in these smaller cells.

EXAMPLE SYLLABLES

짜   쨔   쩌   쪄   쪼   쬬   쭈   쮸   쯔   찌

jja   jjya   jjeo   jjyeo   jjo   jjyo   jju   jjyu   jjeu   jji

DRILLS	Combine these consonants with vowel 애 애							DESCRIBE THE SOUND
ㄱ								
ㅋ								
ㄴ								
ㄷ								
ㅌ								
ㄹ								

DRILLS	Combine these consonants with vowel 애 애							DESCRIBE THE SOUND
ㅁ								
ㅂ								
ㅍ								
ㅅ								
ㅈ								
ㅊ								

NOTE: EXAMPLES ARE FOR WRITING PRACTICE AND MIGHT NOT BE COMMON

DRILLS	Combine these consonants with vowel 에 예								DESCRIBE THE SOUND
ㄱ									
ㅋ									
ㄴ									
ㄷ									
ㅌ									
ㄹ									

DRILLS	Combine these consonants with vowel 예 예								DESCRIBE THE SOUND
ㅁ									
ㅂ									
ㅍ									
ㅅ									
ㅈ									
ㅊ									

(See Reference Charts - Page 123)

DRILLS	Combine these consonants with vowel 외 **외**							DESCRIBE THE SOUND
ㄱ								
ㅋ								
ㄴ								
ㄷ								
ㅌ								
ㄹ								

DRILLS	Combine these consonants with vowel 와 **와**							DESCRIBE THE SOUND
ㅁ								
ㅂ								
ㅍ								
ㅅ								
ㅈ								
ㅊ								

NOTE: EXAMPLES ARE FOR WRITING PRACTICE AND MIGHT NOT BE COMMON

DRILLS	Combine these consonants with vowel 왜 왜							DESCRIBE THE SOUND
ㄱ								
ㅋ								
ㄴ								
ㄷ								
ㅌ								
ㄹ								

DRILLS	Combine these consonants with vowel 위 위							DESCRIBE THE SOUND
ㅁ								
ㅂ								
ㅍ								
ㅅ								
ㅈ								
ㅊ								

(See Reference Charts - Page 123)

DRILLS   Combine these consonants with vowel **워 워**   DESCRIBE THE SOUND

ㄱ

ㅋ

ㄴ

ㄷ

ㅌ

ㄹ

DRILLS   Combine these consonants with vowel **웨 웨**   DESCRIBE THE SOUND

ㅁ

ㅂ

ㅍ

ㅅ

ㅈ

ㅊ

NOTE: EXAMPLES ARE FOR WRITING PRACTICE AND MIGHT NOT BE COMMON

DRILLS	Combine these consonants with vowel 의 **의**						DESCRIBE THE SOUND
ㄱ							
ㅋ							
ㄴ							
ㄷ							
ㅌ							
ㄹ							

DRILLS	Combine the vowels below with an initial ㄲ **ㄲ**						DESCRIBE THE SOUND
야							
요							
오							
이							
유							
어							

(See Reference Charts - Page 123)

DRILLS	Combine the vowels below with an initial ㄸ ㄸ							DESCRIBE THE SOUND
아								
우								
으								
여								
애								
왜								

DRILLS	Combine the vowels below with an initial ㅃ ㅃ							DESCRIBE THE SOUND
외								
애								
위								
예								
여								
유								

NOTE: EXAMPLES ARE FOR WRITING PRACTICE AND MIGHT NOT BE COMMON

DRILLS	Combine the vowels below with an initial ㅆ ㅆ							DESCRIBE THE SOUND
야								
요								
오								
이								
유								
어								

DRILLS	Combine the vowels below with an initial ㅉ ㅉ							DESCRIBE THE SOUND
위								
야								
유								
왜								
여								
의								

(See Reference Charts - Page 123)

QUICK QUIZ! B

Let's put your memory to the test!

1  This letter sounds like ____ ?

A. the **'e'** in hem
B. the **'wo'** in wok
C. the **'gh'** in ghost
D. the **'ye'** in yes

2 How many Hangul diphthongs are there?

A. 10   B. 11
C. 12   D. 13

3 Which of these syllable blocks are wrong?

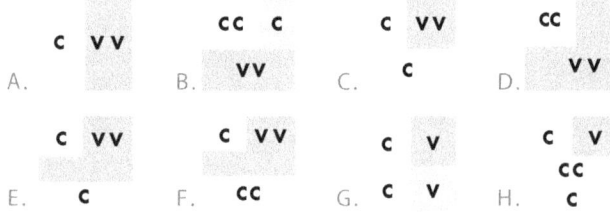

4 Pick the correct spelling for **kiwi** fruit:

A. 그외   B. 지위
C. 키위   D. 끼외

5  This letter sounds like ____ ?

A. the **'wee'** in week
B. the **'we'** in west
C. the **'wo'** in wok
D. the **'wai'** in wait

6  How many strokes does it take to draw this character?

Can you draw the order on the image?

A. 6   B. 8
C. 10   D. 12

7 ____ is pronounced as an **'ae'** sound?

A. ㅖ   B. ㅒ
C. ㅐ   D. ㅔ

8 Which of these double consonant letters sounds like the **'b'** in bananas?

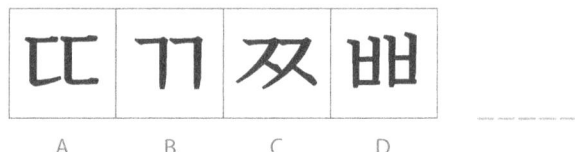

A.   B.   C.   D.

9 Can you work out what a **컴퓨터** is?

A. **comedian**   B. **comforter**
C. **computer**   D. **company**

10  Can you write **hangeul**?

(See Answers - Page 128)

Part 5
COMPLEX & FINAL CONSONANTS
받침

'FINAL' CONSONANTS

We briefly touched upon 받침 **batchim** *(final consonants)* earlier when looking at how we build syllables. They are simply consonants that have an alternate pronunciation when at the bottom of a syllable. Any syllable that has at least 3 letters can have 받침 and they can be either single or double letters.

Being a feature that is unique to the Korean language, 받침 are hard to fully explain in English so it is no surprise that they are often one of the more difficult concepts for beginners to grasp. We will try to simplify things in this chapter.

BATCHIM & GYEOBBATCHIM

Single letter 받침 look just like regular consonants but have the altered pronunciation. Two consonants occupying the bottom space in a syllable are called **gyeobbatchim** 겹받침 *(double final consonants)*.

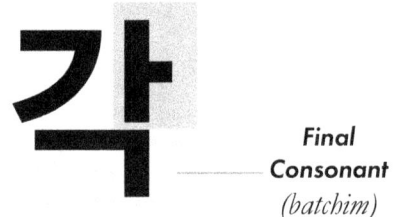
Final Consonant (batchim)

The 겹받침 are **11 new combination consonants** to learn, made with the basic letters again: ㄳ ㄵ ㄶ ㄺ ㄻ ㄼ ㄽ ㄾ ㄿ ㅀ and ㅄ. Unlike the double *'matching'* consonants we learned about earlier, these letters are **only used at the bottom of a syllable** and never anywhere else

Double Final Consonant (gyeobbatchim)

> *In the spirit of keeping things simple,* the easiest way to explain 받침 is that they are all pronounced in one of seven ways - using the sounds associated with seven of the basic Hangul consonants: ㄱ ㄴ ㄷ ㄹ ㅁ ㅂ and ㅇ *(see chart on Page 99).*

IMPORTANT TIP!

The way we pronounce the final consonant sounds requires extra attention and practice. In English, final consonants like the *'-p'* in *'chop'* are usually **aspirated**, with a small blast of air from the mouth, at the end of a word. 받침 letters are not released this way in Korean - practice suppressing that release of air for more accurate 받침 pronunciation.

The complex consonants of 겹받침 contain two letters but we *usually* pronounce just one of them - it depends on whether the syllable is joined to another or not, and whether that that next syllable begins with a vowel or consonant.

When ending a word or followed by a syllable that begins with a consonant, pronounce only the first sound for letters ㄳ ㄵ ㄶ ㄾ ㄽ ㄾ ㅀ and ㅄ. Instead, for the remaining letters ㄺ ㄻ and ㄿ, we take only the second sound. It will be easier to remember the three for which we pronounce the second consonant, instead of memorizing them all!

A different rule applies to all single and double 받침 that are followed by an adjoining, initial vowel. Sounds begin to get carried over from one syllable to the next, creating smoother sounds and easing pronunciation. *Do not worry - we will learn more about this later!*

This is the very last group of letters we need to learn:

ㄳ ㄳ k		
	SAY	Pronounce the **first** letter with the *final* ㄱ sound
ㄳ	STYLES	ㄳ ㄳ ㄳ ㄳ ㄳ ㄳ
	WRITE	Draw **giyeok + siot** with 3 strokes in total.
	IN USE	삯 wages, fee 몫 share, portion
		sags *mogs*

PRACTICE   Trace and draw this letter in the cells below.

ᆬ ᆬ n

SAY — Pronounce the **first** letter with the *final* ㄴ sound

STYLES — ᆬ ᆫᄌ ᆬ ᆬ ᆬ ᆬ

WRITE — Draw **nieun + jieut** with 4 strokes in total.

IN USE — 앉다 to sit   앉으세요 please sit down
anjda   *anjeuseyo*

PRACTICE   Trace and draw this letter in the cells below.

ᆭ ᆭ n

SAY — Pronounce the **first** letter with the *final* ㄴ sound

STYLES — ᆭ ᆫᅘ ᆭ ᆭ ᆭ ᆭ

WRITE — Draw **nieun + hieut** with 4 strokes in total.

IN USE — 많다 many
manhda

PRACTICE   Trace and draw this letter in the cells below.

ㄺ ㄺ k

SAY Pronounce the **second** letter with the *final* ㄱ sound

STYLES ㄺ ㄺ ㄺ ㄺ ㄺ ㄺ

WRITE Draw **rieul + giyeok** with 4 strokes in total.

IN USE 읽다 to read   닭이 chickens
ilgda   *dalgi*

PRACTICE Trace and draw this letter in the cells below.

ㄻ ㄻ m

SAY Pronounce the **second** letter with the *final* ㅁ sound

STYLES ㄻ ㄻ ㄻ ㄻ ㄻ ㄻ

WRITE Draw **rieul + mieum** with 6 strokes in total.

IN USE 삶 life   젊다 to be young
salm   *jeolmda*

PRACTICE Trace and draw this letter in the cells below.

래 래 1

SAY	Pronounce the **first** letter with the *final* ㄹ sound

STYLES	래 ㄹㅂ 래 ㄹㅂ 래 ㄹㅂ
WRITE	Draw **rieul + bieup** with 7 strokes in total.
IN USE	**짧은** short **넓다** to be wide, spacious
	jjalbeun *neolbda*

PRACTICE   Trace and draw this letter in the cells below.

랏 랏 1

SAY	Pronounce the **first** letter with the *final* ㄹ sound

STYLES	랏 ㄹㅅ 랏 ㄹㅅ 랏 ㄹㅅ
WRITE	Draw **rieul + siot** with 5 strokes in total.
IN USE	**외곬** outside
	oegols

PRACTICE   Trace and draw this letter in the cells below.

ㄹㅌ ㄹㅌ 1

SAY — Pronounce the **first** letter with the *final* ㄹ sound

ㄹㅌ

STYLES — ㄹㅌ ㄹㅌ ㄹㅌ ㄹㅌ ㄹㅌ ㄹㅌ

WRITE — Draw **rieul + tieut** with 6 strokes in total.

IN USE — 핥다 to lick
haltda

PRACTICE — Trace and draw this letter in the cells below.

ㄹㅍ ㄹㅍ p

SAY — Pronounce the **second** letter with the *final* ㅂ sound

ㄹㅍ

STYLES — ㄹㅍ ㄹㅍ ㄹㅍ ㄹㅍ ㄹㅍ ㄹㅍ

WRITE — Draw **rieul + pieup** with 7 strokes in total.

IN USE — 읊다 to recite
eulpda

PRACTICE — Trace and draw this letter in the cells below.

ᆶ ᆶ l

SAY — Pronounce the **first** letter with the *final* ㄹ sound

STYLES — ᆶ ᆶ ᆶ ᆶ ᆶ ᆶ

WRITE — Draw **rieul** + **hieut** with 6 strokes in total.

IN USE — 끓다 to boil *(a liquid)*   앓다 to lose
kkeulhda   *ilhda*

PRACTICE — Trace and draw this letter in the cells below.

ᆹ ᆹ p

SAY — Pronounce the **first** letter with the *final* ㅂ sound

STYLES — ᆹ ᆹ ᆹ ᆹ ᆹ ᆹ

WRITE — Draw **bieup** + **siot** with 6 strokes in total.

IN USE — 값을 price   없다 to not exist, to not have
gabseul   *eobsda*

PRACTICE — Trace and draw this letter in the cells below.

DRILLS   Build syllable blocks with the letters in the left column

DESCRIBE THE SOUND

ㄱ + 아 + ㄳ
ㅁ + 요 + ㄵ
ㅂ + 우 + ㄶ
ㄲ + 이 + ㄹ
ㅍ + 애 + ㄻ
ㅅ + 에 + ㄼ
ㅈ + 야 + ㄽ
ㅃ + 어 + ㄾ
ㅊ + 유 + ㄿ
ㅌ + 여 + ㅀ
ㄹ + 오 + ㅄ
ㄷ + 애 + ㄵ
ㅋ + 으 + ㄻ
ㅆ + 우 + ㄾ

(See Answers - Page 127)

DRILLS   Build syllable blocks with the letters in the left column

DESCRIBE THE SOUND

ㅍ + 야 + ㄻ						
ㅂ + 애 + ㄼ						
ㄹ + 와 + ㄳ						
ㅈ + 유 + ㅯ						
ㅃ + 야 + ㄿ						
ㄴ + 왜 + ㄲ						
ㅎ + 오 + ㅀ						
ㅂ + 이 + ㅄ						
ㅁ + 위 + ㄽ						
ㄸ + 아 + ㄼ						
ㅅ + 우 + ㄾ						
ㄴ + 워 + ㅵ						
ㅉ + 왜 + ㅭ						
ㄷ + 예 + ㄹ						

NOTE: EXAMPLES ARE FOR WRITING PRACTICE AND MIGHT NOT BE COMMON

DRILLS Build syllable blocks with the letters in the left column

						DESCRIBE THE SOUND
ㄱ + 예 + ㄻ						
ㄲ + 와 + ㄼ						
ㅁ + 으 + ㄲ						
ㅋ + 야 + ㄽ						
ㅈ + 애 + ㄾ						
ㅃ + 요 + ㄿ						
ㅊ + 아 + ㅀ						
ㅌ + 유 + ㄾ						
ㅂ + 왜 + ㅄ						
ㅍ + 오 + ㄵ						
ㄹ + 의 + ㄶ						
ㄷ + 이 + ㄺ						
ㅋ + 얘 + ㄻ						
ㅎ + 요 + ㄳ						

(See Answers - Page 127)

QUICK QUIZ! C

Let's put your memory to the test!

1 What sound does ㄳ make?
- A. Like 'g' in gum
- B. Like 'k' in dock
- C. Like 't' in chat
- D. Like 's' in sit

2 How many 겹받침 characters are there?
- A. 7   B. 9
- C. 11   D. 13

3 For which 겹받침 do we pronounce the second letter at the end of a word?

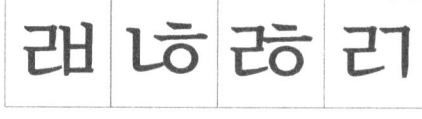

A.   B.   C.   D.

4 There are ___ simplified 받침 sounds?
- A. 8   B. 7
- C. 6   D. 5

5 What sound does ㄹ make?
- A. Like 'm' in men
- B. Like 's' in sing
- C. Like 'l' in laugh
- D. No sound

6 What sound does ㄺ make?
- A. Like 'g' in gum
- B. Like 'k' in dock
- C. Like 'l' in laugh
- D. Like 'r' in run

7 The correct **pronunciation** of 맑게 is :
- A. [말께]   B. [마께]
- C. [말게]   D. [마게]

8 Followed by a syllable with an initial vowel, which sounds like the 'k' in kite?

A.   B.   C.   D.

9 The correct **pronunciation** of 값을 is :
- A. [갓블]   B. [가블]
- C. [가쁠]   D. [갑슬]

10 What sound does ㄹ make?
- A. Like 'm' in men
- B. Like 's' in sing
- C. Like 'l' in laugh
- D. No sound

(See Answers - Page 128)

Part 6

SOUND CHANGE RULES

SOUND CHANGES

Korean words are usually made with more than one syllable block and sentences naturally contain many more. As we begin to join syllables together, certain letter combinations produce different sounds as we try to articulate them - this happens when our articulation speeds up to make conversation. It happens in our native language regularly, occurring without any thought, but is something that we need to learn with a new language and different sound or letter combinations.

To make everyday speech more natural feeling and to generally ease our pronunciations, there a number of **sound change rules** that we need to learn about. The rules describe the changes that take place where these specific letter and syllable combinations meet and written words are spelled differently to the way they sound in speech and conversation.

Throughout this chapter, we will be looking at a series of sound change rules that may not be entirely relevant to beginners. This information will seem much more intense than the previous chapters where we simply learned the Hangul alphabet. Bookmark these pages to return to when you come across any confusing pronunciations.

The bad news for beginners is that these rules simply have to be memorized. They might seem numerous and overwhelming at first but, when you understand where they are used and even put them into practice, you will discover that they will help you pronounce Korean more naturally - they can even assist in developing a more native accent!

SPELLING VS. PRONUNCIATION

약 & 약 = *same pronunciation* | 짚 & 집 = *same pronunciation*

Those who learn English as a foreign language encounter sound changes from spelling to pronunciation with words that we use every day. Consider *'way'* and *'weigh'* - pronounced the same but clearly different words. We tell them apart by how they are spelled or through the context in which they are said. The spelling has to be retained so that we can understand the origin of the word any deeper meaning behind it.

Sound Changes

ASSIMILATION

This is where a final consonant from one syllable interacts with the initial letter in the next syllable, changing how either or both sounds. In isolation, syllables and letters act just as you expect, with the sounds that you have learned each Hangul letter represents. It is when they are spoken together in words, at a normal speed, that sounds assimilate.

Some of the rules are quite broad while others can quite specific - even dictating how just one letter should be pronounced in a very particular scenario. As an example, here is the first of the many sound change rules we will look at together in this chapter:

ㄴ+ㄹ OR ㄹ+ㄴ = ㄹ+ㄹ

연락 → 열락

Spelling   Pronunciation

잘난 → 잘란

① When the letters ㄴ and ㄹ meet between syllables, we pronounce the ㄴ as a ㄹ* sound, making a **double L-sound** *(or '-ll')*. This happens either way around:

② In contrast, when two of the letter ㄹ meet in-between syllables, we always pronounce them as a **single L-sound**.

One example of assimilation with an English word might be *'handbag'* - say it out loud to yourself in a sentence like: *'pass me the handbag, please'*. In casual speech, we would rarely articulate every letter, so it probably sounds closer to '**ham**-*bag*' than '*hand---bag*'.

The assimilated sound is the '*n-*' sound in '*hand*', taking more of an '*m-*' sound as we skip over the '*d-*' sound to say the '*b-*' sound with more speed. Sounds for '*m-*' and '*b-*' are both articulated the same way with our lips (like 'made' & 'bathe') - merging sounds makes the pronunciation easier when talking at a faster rate.

*Exceptions do apply but they are beyond the scope of a starter book like this. For example, when we add a character to an existing word and ㄴ+ㄹ becomes ㄴ+ㄴ.

RE-SYLLABIFICATION

Re-syllabification is a form of assimilation that occurs commonly throughout Korean, changing the way spelled words sound when certain letters meet and interact. These rules are applied broadly, unless an exception is noted:

① When syllables with 받침 are followed by a syllable that starts with a vowel sound, we **carry the final consonant sound over**.

Exceptions: Syllables ending with ㅇ *(ng)* do not change or carry over. If a syllable ends with the letter ㅎ, the '-h' is weakened or practically dropped*.

Remembering that syllable blocks starting with a vowel have ㅇ at the front, the overall effect is ㅇ gets replaced. First, we will examine the Korean word for music:

옷을 → 오슬   책을 → 채글

앞이 → 아피   질문이 → 질무니

꽃을 → 꼬츨   알았어요 → 아라써요

You may not have thought about it before, but we practice re-syllabification all the time when speaking English. Say the phrase 'thank you' out loud to yourself. Did you separate the two words 'thank' and 'you'? It is likely that you pronounced it something along the lines of 'than--kyou' instead. *This is exactly the same concept!*

---

*We may drop the ㅎ sounds between syllables but if letter ㅎ meets certain consonants, it can still have an effect on the way we pronounce the following consonants, strengthening or aspirating them - more on this shortly!

Sound Changes

겹받침 follow some of their own special rules. Not all of this will be relevant to the beginner right away, and the more complex rules are picked up over time. It is important that you are at least aware of them for now.

Generally, only one of the two letters in 겹받침 should be heard when 4-letter syllables are pronounced. This is **normally the first** of the two consonants and applies most when we see the syllable presented in isolation. Here are the other basic rules:

② When double 받침 are followed by syllables starting with a vowel, **both** consonants are pronounced - the double letter is split and we carry the sound of the 2nd consonant over, effectively replacing letter ㅇ.

Spelling   Pronunciation

읽어 → 일거

MEANING: *read*

값을 → 갑슬

MEANING: *price, cost*

삶에 → 살메

MEANING: *life, living*

③ When 겹받침 are followed by a syllable that starts with a consonant, or it is the last syllable in a word, then we then pronounce **only one of the two** consonants.

For ㄹㅁ, ㄹㅍ, and ㄹㄱ, we *usually* say the second consonant - for all other double final consonants, we pronounce the sound from the first of the small letters.

Exceptions: If ㄹㄱ is followed by ㄱ as an initial consonant, we pronounce the ㄹ sound instead.

넋 → 넉   값 → 갑   삶 → 삼

Remember, these rules only apply to the pronunciation of syllables and words. Spellings never change - just the way we say certain combinations of letters, in certain positions.

NASALIZATION

Another assimilation rule that specifically governs letter combinations pronounced with a nasal sound. Any consonants that are followed by letters with the nasal sounds, ㄴ and ㅁ ('-n' and -m' sounds), get converted into more nasal sounds too.

We have created a table *(below)* summarizing the various sound changes for reference. Some examples are provided to help you identify sound changes, but practice is the key:

Final consonant as spelled/written	Followed by letter:	Assimilated sound, batchim to nasal	Pronunciation change with example word
ㄱ ㅋ ㄲ	+ ㄴ	ㄱ → ㅇ	죽는 → 중는
ㄱ	+ ㅁ	ㄱ → ㅇ	국물 → 궁물
ㅂ ㅍ	+ ㄴ	ㅂ → ㅁ	밥맛 → 밤맛
ㅂ ㅍ	+ ㅁ	ㅂ → ㅁ	앞문 → 암문
ㄷ ㅌ ㅈ ㅊ ㅅ ㅆ ㅎ	+ ㄴ / + ㅁ	ㄷ → ㄴ	몇년 → 면년 있는 → 인는 듣는 → 든는

Occurring naturally with English words, it is easy to forget rules like this as you learn a new language - instead, pronouncing syllables with exact phonetics for every letter. Without applying the rules above, the Korean pronunciation you develop could be awkward and quite far from native - *so they are certainly worth memorizing properly!*

Sound Changes

PALATALIZATION

This is where a completely new sound is made when pronouncing specific combinations of letters. It is another sound change that can be tricky to explain but it is also relatively uncommon in everyday Korean conversations and speech.

Sound changes like this tend to occur quite naturally as we try to properly articulate the correct individual sounds in quick succession - *you may find the same with your Korean anyway!*

Once more, an example in English might illustrate this better to begin with: say the phrase *'did you?'* out loud to yourself at a normal conversational speed. Was your pronunciation a highly articulated *'did---you'* or was it actually closer to *'di---jyu'*? Try saying it at different speeds - can you hear and feel how the sounds combine to create a new sound that is missing from the spelling?

Consider how equivalent letters in your own language change sound like these examples:

① ㄷ + 이 → 지

When final consonant ㄷ meets 이, it becomes a ㅈ sound. The silent vowel placeholder is replaced, making a 지 sound.

굳이 → 구지
해돋이 → 해도지

② ㅌ + 이 → 치

If final consonant ㅌ meets 이 it changes to a ㅊ sound. The ㅇ is again effectively replaced to create a 치 sound overall.

같이 → 가치
밭이 → 바치

③ ㄷ + 히 → 치

Another 치 sound is created when ㄷ meets 히, except this time it is consonant ㅎ that we drop to make the new sound.

묻히 → 무치
닫히다 → 다치다

SOUND CHANGES WITH ㅎ

Letter ㅎ is weakened and often inaudible *(especially to non-native speakers)* when between vowels or following voiced, more nasal consonants ㄴ, ㄹ, ㅁ, and ㅇ. For this reason, it is *incorrectly* described as a 'silent' letter - it does seem to get dropped altogether when we hear Koreans speak but, if pronunciation is slowed, it can be heard - it is just very weak.

좋아요 → 조아요   공부하다 → 공부아다
(means - is good)   *(means - to study)*

Advanced: as the most widely used verb form, you will see words with 하다 *quite frequently. It is uncommon to hear this pronounced as it reads, instead sounding more like* 아다.

ASPIRATION

When consonants ㄱ, ㄷ, ㅂ, and ㅈ meet the letter ㅎ, before and after, they take on their much stronger, aspirated sounds *(ㅋ, ㅌ, ㅍ, and ㅊ respectively)*. An extra blast of air is required to pronounce aspirated consonants and when combined with ㅎ *(an aspirated consonant itself)*, we are provided the additional force needed to make that sound:

Examples:

❶ ㅎ + ㄱ → ㅋ
　 ㅎ + ㄷ → ㅌ
　 ㅎ + ㅂ → ㅍ
　 ㅎ + ㅈ → ㅊ

좋고 → 조코
닿다 → 다타
좋지 → 조치
어떻게 → 어떠케

❷ ㄱ + ㅎ → ㅋ
　 ㄷ + ㅎ → ㅌ
　 ㅂ + ㅎ → ㅍ
　 ㅈ + ㅎ → ㅊ

국화 → 구콰
집회 → 지풰
맞히다 → 마치다

'INTENSIFICATION' & 'REINFORCEMENT'

When consonants are written adjacent to one another, they can often interact to cause changes that make the overall pronunciation easier. This set of rules refer to a range of phonetic changes with lots of consistencies and plenty of exceptions. Not only does this make it hard to fully describe but, as you can imagine, incredibly difficult to grasp when you are trying to learn Korean!

What makes it trickier is that most native Koreans would not learn to speak using rules like this - instead, they would simply adopt them in a more organic way. *Confused yet?*

In basic terms, when a syllable ends with certain consonants, and an adjoining syllable starts with either ㄱ,ㄷ,ㅂ,ㅅ, or ㅈ, their sounds doubles in strength = ㄲ,ㄸ,ㅃ,ㅆ,ㅉ.

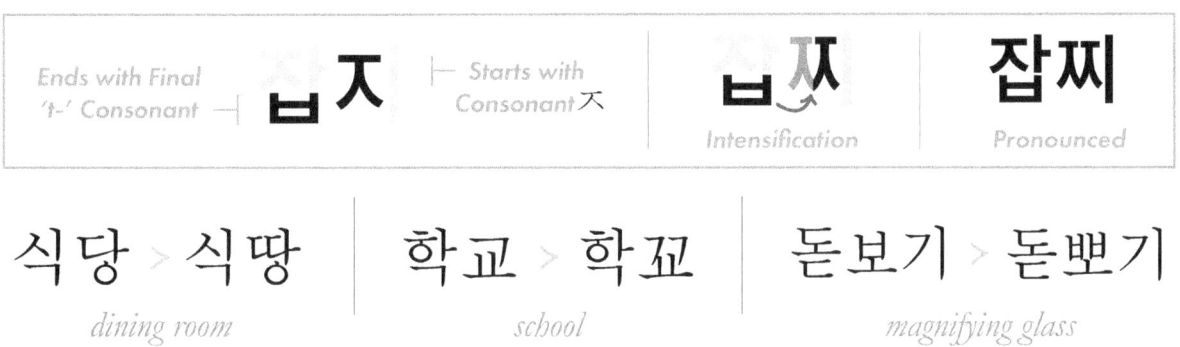

식당 > 식땅 | 학교 > 학꾜 | 돋보기 > 돋뽀기
dining room | *school* | *magnifying glass*

To shorten 받침 sounds like ㅂ at the end of a word or isolated syllable, we suppress the release of air that normally follows these types of letters - the aspiration. To illustrate, hold your hand in front of your face and say the words *'tar'* and *'star'* - did you feel a little blast of air from the *'t-'* in *'tar'* but not from the one in *'star'*?

When we encounter one of these reinforcing consonants, we can convert any built-up force from suppressing aspiration in 받침 to intensify the sound of the following letter. It becomes a shorter, higher pitched version, with a more explosive burst of air.

Note: Final consonant ㅎ only intensifies an initial ㅅ, making it a ㅆ sound at the start.

좋습니다 → 조씁니다   MEANING: *good*
Spelling   *Pronunciation*

COMMON EXCEPTIONS

Most rule exceptions are learned simply by reading, writing, and speaking more Korean. There are too many to highlight them all, but here are a few common ones:

① Assimilation exceptions are made when ㅁ or ㅇ in the 받침 position meet ㄹ in an initial position. In both cases, ㄹ is replaced by a ㄴ sound.

ㅁ OR ㅇ + ㄹ   음력 → 음녁   *lunar calendar*

Less common exceptions with consonants acting strangely in front of the letter ㄹ include, for example: letters ㄱ, ㄷ or ㅂ (+ㄹ) becoming ㅇ, ㄴ, and ㅁ (+ㄴ) respectively.

② ㅎ is pronounced as ㄷ in the *final* position but when it meets letter ㄴ as an initial consonant, we pronounce it as another ㄴ:

ㅎ + ㄴ = ㄴ + ㄴ   닿는 → 단는   *touch, reach*

③ Letter ㅅ is pronounced as ㄷ in the *final* position but ㄷ is pronounced as ㅌ when followed by ㅎ. Therefore, when letter ㅅ is followed by ㅎ, it undergoes two sound changes at once and is pronounced as ㅌ:

ㅅ + ㅎ = ㅌ   못하다 → 모타다   *unable to, can't*

④ Letter ㅅ has a 'sh-' sound when paired with the vowels 이 여 야 요 and 유, but instead has a 's-' sound with vowels 아 어 우 오 으 애 or 에:

ㅅ = 's-' OR 'sh-'   샴푸 *shampoo* [syam-pu]   사서 *librarian* [sa-seo]

SIMPLIFICATION

Batchim pronunciation can be simplified to one of seven sounds, as per the table below:

**These letters are never used in the final position as batchim (final consonants).*

Sound Changes

'INTRUSIVE' ㄴ

There is an unexpected ㄴ sound that we occasionally hear in Korean. It could perhaps be compared to the way some English words are pronounced with sounds that do not fit their spellings - like the '-ff' sound in the word 'rough'. While this is not the same, it may help to illustrate what type of sound change the phenomenon of 'intrusive ㄴ' is!

It is an interesting rule that beginners probably do not need to learn, but it shows up and is worth understanding. In special circumstances, the ㄴ sound can show up and ease pronunciations not covered by other rules - in particular, as we will see here, it is added when some composite words are said - *two words joined together to create new meaning.*

꽃잎 → 꼰닙   MEANING: *petal*

This is a fantastic example of a compound word that we pronounce with this rule - the two separate words it contains are *flower* 꽃 and *leaf* 잎.

Intrusive ㄴ pronunciation occurs when both characters are words in their own right - like in the example above. The first word must also end with 받침 *(letter* ㅊ *here)*, and the second word must begin with one of five specific vowels ㅣ ㅑ ㅕ ㅛ or ㅠ.

We can see that the correctly spelled version *(left)* looks vastly different to the *pronounced* version *(transcribed on the right)*. There are a series of sound change rules working at the same time in this example - here is a little breakdown:

꽃잎 → 꽃닢 → 꼰닢 → 꼰닙
Spelling   + ㄴ Rule   Nasalization   Simplification

Note: If the end consonant is letter ㄹ, we pronounce this additional ㄴ as ㄹ instead.

As a foreigner, you would be understood perfectly well if a rule like passes you by - the intrusive ㄴ should not be worried about too much as a beginner. *It is quite advanced!*

Part 7

USEFUL WORDS & BEGINNER VOCABULARY

NUMBERS

There are **two number systems** in Korean and they are both regularly used in everyday life - *so we need to learn both!* The first system is called **Sino-Korean** and the second can be referred to as *'pure* Korean' or **'native Korean'**. The two systems have different uses, depending on the situation, and they are even combined in some contexts.

Sino-Korean is a term that describes elements of the Korean language that are either influenced by, or originated in, China. Almost two thirds of Korean vocabulary is considered Sino-Korean and it can be written either with Hangul or a different alphabet, called *Hanja (Chinese characters)*.

The Korean number systems can sound quite complex but both work with familiar logic and only a relatively small group of words are needed to make every number we need.

#	'Native' Korean		Sino-Korean	
0	영*	[yeong]	공*	[gong]
1	하나	[ha-na]	일	[il]
2	둘	[dul]	이	[i]
3	셋	[set]	삼	[sam]
4	넷	[net]	사	[sa]
5	다섯	[da-seot]	오	[o]
6	여섯	[yeo seot]	육	[yuk]
7	일곱	[il-gop]	칠	[chil]
8	여덟	[yeo-deol]	팔	[pal]
9	아홉	[a-hop]	구	[gu]
10	열	[yeol]	십	[sip]

How each system is generally used:

Sino-Korean

- Time *(minutes only)*
- Addresses
- Phone Numbers
- Sports/Scores
- Money
- Dates
- Measurement
- ...anything else!

Native Korean

- Time *(hours only)*
- Counting People
- Counting Objects
- Sequences
- Ages

Notes:

'Native Korean' numbers end at 99 so *Sino-Korean* numbers are at 100 and higher.

Native Korean numbers can also have slightly different forms as adjectives, but the words shown here are perfectly adequate for almost any context.

Both versions of zero are Hanja, derived from Chinese - we tend to use 공 for Sino-Korean numbers.

Vocabulary & Revision

Sino-Korean numbers quite easy to learn! Once you have memorized the numbers 1-10, we create most bigger numbers by simply combining those with the words for larger, round numbers such as 10, 100, 1000, and so on. There are no composite words between 19 and 100, such as 'twenty' or 'thirty', and we would say 'two-ten' or 'three-ten' instead. In effect, single digits in front of large numbers multiply, and those following are added:

2	이	*two*
12	십이	*ten--two*
20	이십	*two--ten*
22	이십이	*two--ten--two*
200	이백	*two--hundred*
202	이백이	*two--hundred-------------two*
212	이백십이	*two--hundred---------ten--two*
220	이백이십	*two--hundred--two--ten*
222	이백이십이	*two--hundred--two--ten--two*

10	십
100	백
1,000	천
10,000	만
100,000	십만
1,000,000	백만
10,000,000	천만

...larger numbers are also multiplied above 10,000

The large, round numbers from 100 and upwards can be expressed in two ways when written on their own - either as 일백 '*one--hundred*' or, more commonly, just 백 '*hundred*'. It is the same for 일천 '*one--thousand*' and 천 '*thousand*' - they are interchangeable.

'Native Korean' numbering only goes to 99 and works slightly differently.

We must learn unique words for each multiple of 10, in addition to the single digit numbers. They are added together, as in the examples in the table to the right, each shown with number 둘 *(2)*:

10	열		12	열둘
20	스물		22	스물둘
30	서른		32	서른둘
40	마흔		40	마흔둘
50	쉰		52	쉰둘
60	예순		62	예순둘
70	일흔		70	일흔둘
80	여든		82	여든둘
90	아흔		92	아흔둘

DRILLS   Practice writing the 'Native' Korean numbers below:

1	하나
2	둘
3	셋
4	넷
5	다섯
6	여섯
7	일곱
8	여덟
9	아홉
10	열
12	열둘
15	열다섯
18	열여덟
19	열아홉

DRILLS   Practice writing the 'Native' Korean numbers below:

20	스물							
30	서른							
40	마흔							
50	쉰							
60	예순							
70	일흔							
80	여든							
90	아흔							
24	스물넷							
57	쉰일곱							
61	예순하나							
73	일흔셋							
86	여든여섯							
92	아흔둘							

DRILLS Practice writing the **Sino-Korean** numbers below:

0	공							
1	일							
2	이							
3	삼							
4	사							
5	오							
6	육							
7	칠							
8	팔							
9	구							
10	십							
100	백							
1,000	천							
10,000	만							

DRILLS   Practice writing the **Sino-Korean** numbers below:

11	공	일							
19	십	구							
23	이	십	삼						
77	칠	십	칠						
125	백	이	십	오					
199	백	구	십	구					
201	이	백	일						
358	삼	백	오	십	팔				
540	오	백	사	십					
999	구	백	구	십	구				
1001	천	일							
2054	이	천	오	십	사				
9,999	구	천	구	백	구	십	구		

DAYS AND MONTHS

Practice writing the Days of the Week below:

The days of the week have *Sino-Korean names*, represented by five natural elements *(from Chinese culture)* and the two heavenly bodies *(sun and moon)*. Calendar months also use Sino-Korean for naming, although they follow the number system we have just learned.

The format when writing a date in Korean is quite familiar - if you were writing your birthday, it would be arranged like this: YYYY년 MM월 DD일 and the number for years can be reduced to two digits. If you can learn the Sino Korean numbers and those words just above for years, days, and months, you can easily write any date you like - Hangeul Day falls on October the 9th - that would be 10월 9일 ...*or* 시월 구일, for example.

Notes: 일 means '*day*' in the context below but means '*work*' if used in isolation. The second part of each day's name, 요일, can be seen shortened to just the first syllable. Also, the symbols at the front of each name are not necessarily used as words in other contexts for the same meaning - *e.g., 'sun' is* 태양, *not* 일.

Tip: Western days of the week end with '*-day*' and Korean ones end with '-요일' *(yo-il)*.

MONDAY 월 MOON	월	요	일					
TUESDAY 화 FIRE	화	요	일					
WEDNESDAY 수 WATER	수	요	일					
THURSDAY 목 WOOD	목	요	일					
FRIDAY 금 GOLD	금	요	일					
SATURDAY 토 EARTH	토	요	일					
SUNDAY 일 SUN/DAY	일	요	일					

Practice writing the Months of the year below:

The names of months are simply Sino-Korean numbers with the word 월 *(wol)*, meaning month, e.g. 1월 is *January*, 2월 is *February*, and so on. Two exceptions (marked *) have slight alterations that ease pronunciation: *June is* 유월 *not* 육월 & *October* 시월 *not* 십월.

JANUARY 1월	일 월	
FEBRUARY 2월	이 월	
MARCH 3월	삼 월	
APRIL 4월	사 월	
MAY 5월	오 월	
JUNE * 6월	유 월	
JULY 7월	칠 월	
AUGUST 8월	팔 월	
SEPTEMBER 9월	구 월	
OCTOBER * 10월	시 월	
NOVEMBER 11월	십 일 월	
DECEMBER 12월	십 이 월	

COLORS

After memorizing the alphabet and learning about numbers and dates, a useful and easy next step with any new language is usually to learn how to write and say the colors.

The words in the following lists can generally be used as and nouns. You will quickly notice that they all end with 색 *(saek)* - a short version of 색깔 *(saekkkal)* - which is the Korean word for 'color'. We use the short word 색 when we are talking about a specific color but, in some cases, where certain colors are used as adjectives, this can be omitted if you like. *Those colors are marked with* *

Practice writing the colors below:

RED *	빨	간	색							
ORANGE	주	황	색							
YELLOW *	노	란	색							
GREEN	초	록	색							
BLUE *	파	란	색							
PURPLE	보	라	색							
PINK	분	홍	색							
WHITE *	하	얀	색							
BLACK *	검	정	색							
GRAY	회	색								

Practice writing some more Korean color words below:

GOLD	금	색								
SILVER	은	색								
BRONZE	청	동	색							
BROWN	갈	색								
NAVY BLUE	곤	색								
SKY BLUE	하	늘	색							
DARK GREEN	초	록								
LIGHT GREEN	연	두	색							
TURQUOISE	청	록	색							
TAN	황	갈	색							
JADE	비	취	색							
BEIGE	베	이	지	색						
PEACH	복	숭	아	색						
RAINBOW	무	지	개	색						

VOCABULARY LISTS

The following series of pages contain a selection of basic vocabulary lists, curated by theme. Memorizing vocabulary is a highly underrated task for beginners learning Korean. In addition to mastering the Hangul alphabet, having a good knowledge of everyday words will go a long way when you progress to more advanced levels. It's important to remember that a good vocabulary is needed when you come to learn more about grammar and start forming real sentences. Try copying words into new lists - both repetition and personal curation goes a long way when memorizing new vocabulary. *There are pages of extra practice grid paper towards the back of this book that you can photocopy for personal use.*

FOOD 음식 & EATING 먹기

식사	meal
아침(식사)	breakfast
점심(식사)	lunch
저녁(식사)	dinner
과자	snack
고기	meat
돼지고기	pork
소고기	beef
닭고기	chicken
해물	seafood
재료	ingredients
김치	kimchi
반찬	side dish
식당	restaurant
메뉴	menu
젓가락	chopsticks
칼	knife
포크	fork
숟가락	spoon
도마	cutting board

접시	plate
그릇	bowl
냄비	pot
탁자	table
음료수	beverage
물	water
콜라	cola
맥주	beer
사이다	cider
켄	can
병	bottle
우유	milk
냉면	cold noodles
밥	rice
볶음밥	fried rice
만두	dumplings
어묵	fishcake
전	pancake

FRUITS 과일 & VEGETABLES 채소

사과	*apple*	바나나	*banana*
오렌지	*orange*	파파야	*papaya*
귤	*tangerine*	마늘	*garlic*
승도복숭아	*nectarine*	양파	*onion*
포도	*grapes*	당근	*carrot*
배	*pear*	감자	*potato*
멜론	*melon*	고구마	*sweet potato*
수박	*watermelon*	브로콜리	*broccoli*
레몬	*lemon*	버섯	*mushroom*
라임	*lime*	양배추	*cabbage*
딸기	*strawberry*	완두콩	*peas*
산딸기	*raspberry*	옥수수	*corn*
블루베리	*blueberry*	부추	*leek*
블랙베리	*blackberry*	순무	*turnip*
크랜베리	*cranberry*	호박	*pumpkin*
체리	*cherry*	토마토	*tomato*
복숭아	*peach*	상추	*lettuce*
살구	*apricot*	오이	*cucumber*
자두	*plum*	피망	*bell pepper*
키위	*kiwi*	셀러리	*celery*
망고	*mango*	아보카도	*avocado*
파인애플	*pineapple*	샐러드	*salad*
자몽	*grapefruit*	올리브	*olive*
석류	*pomegranate*	애호박	*zucchini*
코코넛	*coconut*	껍질콩	*green beans*
피타야	*dragon fruit*	무	*radish*
두리안	*durian*	견과	*nut*
대추	*jujube*	아몬드	*almond*
금귤	*kumquat*	땅콩	*peanut*

SHOPPING 쇼핑 & CLOTHES 옷

식료품	grocery	사다	to buy
가게	store/shop	바지	pants
약국	pharmacy	청바지	jeans
빵집	bakery	모자	hat
열림 / 닫힘	open/closed	반바지	shorts
슈퍼마켓	supermarket	치마	skirt
쇼핑센터	shopping center	양말	socks
백화점	department store	신발	shoes
(전통)시장	(traditional) market	원피스	dress
편의점	convenience store	운동화	sneakers
서점	bookstore	양복	suit
꽃집	flower shop	안경	glasses
영업시간	opening hours	셔츠	shirt
돈	money	하이힐	high heels
현금	cash	티셔츠	t-shirt
신용 카드	credit card	재킷	jacket
체크 카드	debit card	드레스	dress
할인	discount	파자마	pyjama
반값	half price	브라	bra
싸다	cheap	팬티	underwear
저렴하다	inexpensive	코트	coat
가격표	price tag	구두	dress shoe
기념품	souvenirs		
보증서	warranty		
환불	refund		
교환	exchange		
영수증	receipt		
세금	tax		
쿠폰	coupon		

WEATHER 날씨 & TRAVEL 여행

기온	temperature	맑다	clear
여름	summer	쌀쌀하다	chilly
겨울	winter	영하	below zero
가을	fall	영상	above zero
봄	spring	기후	climate
하늘	sky	국내 여행	local trip
구름	clouds	해외 여행	overseas trip
이슬비	drizzle	비행기	airplane
눈바람	blizzard	공항	airport
비	rain	해외	foreign country
눈	snow	버스	bus
번개	lightning	버스 정류장	bus stop
천둥	thunder	역	station
소나기	shower	버스 정류장	bus station
태풍	typhoon	여권	passport
우산	umbrella	지하철	subway
비옷	rain jacket	택시	taxi
장마	rainy season	입장시간	opening time
해	sun	마감시간	closing time
가뭄	drought	숙소	accommodation
자외선	UV rays	짐	baggage
해변	beach	지도	map
바다	ocean	관광 가이드	tour guide
에어컨	air conditioner	표	ticket
공기	air	다리	bridge
바람	wind	바다	sea
폭염	heat wave	등대	lighthouse
건조하다	dry	해변	beach
습하다	humid	산	mountain

HOUSE 집 & HOME 가정

아파트	apartment
방	room
바닥	floor
천장	ceiling
일층	first floor
지하실	basement
다락방	attic
계단	stairs
정원	garden
창문	window
식물	plant
화분	flowerpot
주방 / 부엌	kitchen
싱크대	sink (kitchen)
세탁기	washing machine
마이크로웨이브	microwave
냉장고	refrigerator
냉동고	freezer
난로	stove
식기세척기	dishwasher
오븐	oven
주전자	kettle
토스터	toaster
컵	cup
벽장	cupboard
후라이팬	frying pan
냄비	pot
거실	living room
가구	furniture
티비	TV
텔레비전	television
소파	sofa
의자	chair
탁자	table
식탁	dining table
책장	bookshelf
라디오	radio
그림	picture
페인팅	painting
침실	bedroom
침대	bed
베개	pillow
자명종	alarm clock
옷장	wardrobe
깔개	rug
램프	lamp
전구	light bulb
거울	mirror
포스터	poster
책상	desk
컴퓨터	computer
화장실	bathroom
변기	toilet
샤워	shower
욕조	bathtub
싱크	sink
약상자	medicine cabinet

BODY 몸

머리	head		가슴	chest
이마	forehead		등	back
눈	eye		허리	waist
귀	ear		배꼽	navel
귓불	earlobe		다리	leg
코	nose		허벅지	thigh
입	mouth		무릎	knee
입술	lips		종아리	calf
혀	tongue		발	foot
볼/뺨	cheek		발목	ankle
이/치아	tooth/teeth		발톱	toenail
턱	chin		발꿈치	heel
목	neck		발바닥	sole
목구멍	throat		발가락	toe
어깨	shoulder		근육	muscle
쇄골	collarbone		뼈	bone
팔	arm		심장	heart
팔목	wrist		피 / 혈액	blood
팔꿈치	elbow		위	stomach
손	hand		머리카락	hair
손바닥	palm of hand		수염	facial hair
주먹	fist		콧수염	moustache
손가락	finger		눈썹	eyebrow
엄지손가락	thumb		얼굴	face
집게손가락	index finger		피부	skin
약지	ring finger		점	spot
손톱	fingernail		보조개	dimple
중지	middle finger		여드름	pimple
새끼 손가락	pinkie finger		주근깨	freckle

PHONE 전화

메시지	message
지도	map
카메라	camera
사진	photo
갤러리	gallery
시계	clock
미리알림	reminder
캘린더	calendar
주소록	contacts
계산기	calculator
음악	music
소리	sound
방해금지 모드	do not disturb mode
제어 센터	control centre
에어플레인 모드	airplane mode
알림	notification
(홈)화면	(home) screen
잠그화면	lock screen
설정	settings
와이파이	Wi-Fi
개인용 핫스팟	hotspot
이동통신사	mobile network
셀룰러	cellular
모바일 데이터	mobile data
전원 끄기	power off
번역	translator
앱	app
메모리	memory
로그인	login
비밀번호	password
선택	select
복사	copy
붙여넣기	paste
이동	move
지르기	crop
이름 변경	rename
계속	continue
취소	cancel
입력	input
수신함	inbox
오전	am
오후	pm
좋아하다	to like
팔로워	followers
페이지	page
활동	activity
새 포스트	new post
리블로그하다	to repost
임시 저장	drafts
답하기	answer
위치	location
익명으로	anonymous
배터리 전원 부족	low battery

OCCUPATIONS 직업

직장	workplace	바텐더	bartender
경력	career	전기기사	electrician
이력서	CV	경찰	police officer
면접	job interview	소방관	fireman
고용주	employer	배관공	plumber
연봉	annual salary	어부	fisherman
월급	monthly salary	정육점	butcher
동료	colleague	목수	carpenter
회의	meeting	건축가	architect
출장	business trip	조종사	pilot
퇴직자	retiree	약사	pharmacist
선생님	teacher	점원	store clerk
교수님	professor	정원사	gardener
연구원	researcher	수의사	vet
학생	student	미용사	hairdresser
간호사	nurse	운동선수	athlete
치과의사	dentist	노동자	worker/laborer
의사	doctor	수리 기사	repair technician
군인	soldier	사진사	photographer
요리사	cook/chef	프로그래머	programmer
변호사	lawyer	가수	singer
비서	secretary	배우	actor
은행가	banker	사무원	office worker
작가	writer/author	농장주/농부	farmer
기자	journalist	택시기사	taxi driver
엔지니어	engineer	기술자	technician
과학자	scientist	보모	nanny
디자이너	designer	예술가	artist
정비사	mechanic	회계사	accountant

ANIMALS 동물 & INSECTS 벌레

애완동물	pet	오리	duck
개	dog	비둘기	pigeon
강아지	puppy	거위	goose
고양이	cat	독수리	eagle
새	bird	뱀	snake
물고기	fish	북극곰	polar bear
코끼리	elephant	캥거루	kangaroo
사자	lion	돌고래	dolphin
호랑이	tiger	상어	shark
곰	bear	오징어	squid
기린	giraffe	문어	octopus
얼룩말	zebra	게	crab
고릴라	gorilla	장어	eel
원숭이	monkey	나비	butterfly
판다	panda	다람쥐	squirrel
하마	hippo	오소리	badger
코뿔소	rhinoceros	토끼	rabbit
고래	whale	햄스터	hamster
거북이	turtle	기니피그	guinea pig
악어	crocodile	개구리	frog
거미	spider	늑대	wolf
벌	bee	사슴	deer
개미	ant	여우	fox
소	cow	칠면조	turkey
염소	goat	도마뱀	lizard
양	sheep	표범	leopard
말	horse	치타	cheetah
돼지	pig	펭귄	penguin
앵무새	parrot	침팬지	chimpanzee

FAMILY 가족

가족	family
아이들	children
아들	son
딸	daughter
아이	child
부모(님)	parents
어머니	mother (formal)
어머님	mother (honorific)
엄마	mother (informal)
아버지	father (formal)
아버님	father (honorific)
아빠	father (informal)
조부모(님)	grandparents
할아버지	grandfather
할아버님	grandfather (honorific)
할머니	grandmother
할머님	grandmother (honorific)
배우자	spouse
남편	husband
아내	wife
형제자매	siblings (general)
형제	brothers
자매	sisters
누나	older sister (for male)
형	older brother (for male)
언니	older sister (for female)
오빠	older brother (for female)
여동생	younger sister
남동생	younger brother

HOBBIES 취미

여행	travel
외국어	foreign language
요리	cooking
독서	reading
운동	exercise
독서	reading books
영화 감상	watching movies
비디오 게임	video games
스포츠	sports
축구	soccer
야구	baseball
농구	basketball
수영	swimming
조깅	jogging
테니스	tennis
골프	golf
스키	ski
미식축구	football
배구	volleyball
태권도	taekwondo
등산	hiking
달리기	running
춤	dance
가요	K-pop
미술	visual art
낮잠	nap
휴가	vacation
문화	culture
수다	chat

QUICK QUIZ! D

Let's put your memory to the test!

1

사	
구	
이	
칠	

2

8	
3	
5	
1	

3

이십삼	
육십구	
십육	
삼십팔	

4 Approximately how much of Korean vocabulary has Chinese origins?

   A. all B. 1/3
   C. 2/3 D. half

5 What is the Korean for Monday, the day named after the moon?

   A. 화요일 B. 목요일
   C. 일요일 D. 월요일

6 How do we say the name of the 11th month, November, in Korean?

   A. 십일월 B. 삼이월
   C. 십이월 D. 삼일월

7 Which color is written as **파란색**?

   A. blue   B. white
   C. black D. yellow
   E. green F. red

8

사백십육	
팔백십이	
삼백이십일	

9

540	
199	
704	

(Answers on Page 128)

Part 8

REFERENCE CHARTS & ANSWERS

		ㅏ a	ㅑ ya	ㅓ eo	ㅕ yeo	ㅗ o	ㅛ yo	ㅜ u	ㅠ yu	ㅡ eu	ㅣ i
ㄱ	g	가 ga	갸 gya	거 geo	겨 gyeo	고 go	교 gyo	구 gu	규 gyu	그 geu	기 gi
ㅋ	k	카 ka	캬 kya	커 keo	켜 kyeo	코 ko	쿄 kyo	쿠 ku	큐 kyu	크 keu	키 ki
ㄴ	n	나 na	냐 nya	너 neo	녀 nyeo	노 no	뇨 nyo	누 nu	뉴 nyu	느 neu	니 ni
ㄷ	d	다 da	댜 dya	더 deo	뎌 dyeo	도 do	됴 dyo	두 du	듀 dyu	드 deu	디 di
ㅌ	t	타 ta	탸 tya	터 teo	텨 tyeo	토 to	툐 tyo	투 tu	튜 tyu	트 teu	티 ti
ㄹ	r/l	라 ra	랴 rya	러 reo	려 ryeo	로 ro	료 ryo	루 ru	류 ryu	르 reu	리 ri
ㅁ	m	마 ma	먀 mya	머 meo	며 myeo	모 mo	묘 myo	무 mu	뮤 myu	므 meu	미 mi
ㅂ	b	바 ba	뱌 bya	버 beo	벼 byeo	보 bo	뵤 byo	부 bu	뷰 byu	브 beu	비 bi
ㅍ	p	파 pa	퍄 pya	퍼 peo	펴 pyeo	포 po	표 pyo	푸 pu	퓨 pyu	프 peu	피 pi
ㅅ	s	사 sa	샤 sya	서 seo	셔 syeo	소 so	쇼 syo	수 su	슈 syu	스 seu	시 si
ㅈ	j	자 ja	쟈 jya	저 jeo	져 jyeo	조 jo	죠 jyo	주 ju	쥬 jyu	즈 jeu	지 ji
ㅊ	ch	차 cha	챠 chya	처 cheo	쳐 chyeo	초 cho	쵸 chyo	추 chu	츄 chyu	츠 cheu	치 chi
ㅇ	ng -	아 a	야 ya	어 eo	여 yeo	오 o	요 yo	우 u	유 yu	으 eu	이 i
ㅎ	h	하 ha	햐 hya	허 heo	혀 hyeo	호 ho	효 hyo	후 hu	휴 hyu	흐 heu	히 hi

		ㅐ ae	ㅒ yae	ㅔ e	ㅖ ye	ㅚ oe	ㅘ wa	ㅙ wae	ㅟ wi	ㅝ wo	ㅞ we	ㅢ ui
ㄱ	g	개 gae	걔 gyae	게 ge	계 gye	괴 goe	과 gwa	괘 gwae	귀 gwi	궈 gwo	궤 gwe	긔 gui
ㅋ	k	캐 kae	컈 kyae	케 ke	켸 kye	쾨 koe	콰 kaw	쾌 kwae	퀴 kwi	쿼 kwo	퀘 kwe	킈 kui
ㄴ	n	내 nae	냬 nyae	네 ne	녜 nye	뇌 noe	놔 nwa	놰 nwae	뉘 nwi	눠 nwo	눼 nwe	늬 nui
ㄷ	d	대 dae	댸 dyae	데 de	뎨 dye	되 doe	돠 dwa	돼 dwae	뒤 dwi	둬 dwo	뒈 dwe	듸 dui
ㅌ	t	태 tae	턔 tyae	테 te	톄 tye	퇴 toe	톼 twa	퇘 twae	튀 twi	퉈 two	퉤 twe	틔 tui
ㄹ	r/l	래 rae	럐 ryae	레 re	례 rye	뢰 roe	롸 rwa	뢔 rwae	뤼 rwi	뤄 rwo	뤠 rwe	릐 rui
ㅁ	m	매 mae	먜 myae	메 me	몌 mye	뫼 moe	뫄 mwa	뫠 mwae	뮈 mwi	뭐 mwo	뭬 mwe	믜 mui
ㅂ	b	배 bae	뱨 byae	베 be	볘 bye	뵈 boe	봐 bwa	봬 bwae	뷔 bwi	붜 bwo	붸 bwe	븨 bui
ㅍ	p	패 pae	퍠 pyae	페 pe	폐 pye	푀 poe	퐈 pwa	퐤 pwae	퓌 pwi	풔 pwo	풰 pwe	픠 pui
ㅅ	s	새 sae	섀 syae	세 se	셰 sye	쇠 soe	솨 swa	쇄 swae	쉬 swi	숴 swo	쉐 swe	싀 sui
ㅈ	j	재 jae	쟤 jyae	제 je	졔 jye	죄 joe	좌 jwa	좨 jwae	쥐 jwi	줘 jwo	줴 jwe	즤 jui
ㅊ	ch	채 chae	챼 chyae	체 che	쳬 chye	최 choe	촤 chwa	쵀 chwae	취 chwi	춰 chwo	췌 chwe	츼 chui
ㅇ	-ng	애 ae	얘 yae	에 eo	예 ye	외 oe	와 wa	왜 wae	위 wi	워 wo	웨 we	의 ui
ㅎ	h	해 hae	햬 hyae	헤 he	혜 hye	회 hoe	화 hwa	홰 hwae	휘 hwi	훠 hwo	훼 hwe	희 hui

	㗢 ae	㖿 yae	㝠 e	㋋ ye	ㅚ oe	ㅘ wa	ㅙ wae	ㅟ wi	ㅝ wo	ㅞ we	ㅢ ui
ㄲ gg	깨 ggae	꺠 ggyae	께 gge	꼐 ggye	꾀 ggoe	꽈 ggwa	꽤 ggwae	뀌 ggi	꿔 ggwo	꿰 ggwe	끠 ggui
ㄸ dd	때 ddae	떄 ddyae	떼 dde	뗴 ddye	뙤 ddoe	똬 ddwa	뙈 ddwae	뛰 ddi	뚸 ddwo	뛔 ddwe	띄 ddui
ㅃ bb	빼 bbae	뺴 bbyae	뻬 bbe	뼤 bbye	뾔 bboe	뽜 bbwa	뽸 bbwae	쀠 bbi	뿨 bbwo	쀄 bbwe	쁴 bbui
ㅆ ss	쌔 ssae	썌 ssyae	쎄 sse	쎼 ssye	쐬 ssoe	쏴 sswa	쐐 sswae	쒸 ssi	쒀 sswo	쒜 sswe	씌 ssui
ㅉ jj	째 jjae	쨰 jjyae	쩨 jje	쪠 jjye	쬐 jjoe	쫘 jjwa	쫴 jjwae	쮜 jji	쭤 jjwo	쮀 jjwe	찌 jjui

We do not need to memorize every possible character - by simply learning the basic Hangul letters and how they are written, you can read and write all possible combinations.

Note: In theory, there are hundreds upon thousands of possible syllable combinations but a great many of them are rarely used in everyday Korean. In fact, there are lots that never get used at all!

	ㅏ a	ㅑ ya	ㅓ eo	ㅕ yeo	ㅗ o	ㅛ yo	ㅜ u	ㅠ yu	ㅡ eu	ㅣ i
ㄲ gg	까 gga	꺄 ggya	꺼 ggeo	껴 ggyeo	꼬 ggo	꾜 ggyo	꾸 ggu	뀨 ggyu	끄 ggeu	끼 ggi
ㄸ dd	따 dda	땨 ddya	떠 ddeo	뗘 ddyeo	또 ddo	뚀 ddyo	뚜 ddu	뜌 ddyu	뜨 ddeu	띠 ddi
ㅃ bb	빠 bba	뺘 bbya	뻐 bbeo	뼈 bbyeo	뽀 bbo	뾰 bbyo	뿌 bbu	쀼 bbyu	쁘 bbeu	삐 bbi
ㅆ ss	싸 ssa	쌰 ssya	써 sseo	쎠 ssyeo	쏘 sso	쑈 ssyo	쑤 ssu	쓔 ssyu	쓰 sseu	씨 ssi
ㅉ jj	짜 jja	쨔 jjya	쩌 jjeo	쪄 jjyeo	쪼 jjo	쬬 jjyo	쭈 jju	쮸 jjyu	쯔 jjeu	찌 jji

PRACTICE SYLLABLES PAGES 87-89

갓	퍎	곜
뫂	뱮	꽈
붛	뢊	믁
낈	쥪	걍
퍰	뺢	잻
셒	놬	뿊
쟎	홍	찷
뻪	빐	튫
춦	뫾	뵀
텋	땲	폿
룳	숤	릥
댔	늧	딁
큲	쨍	캪
쓭	뎈	효

ANSWERS

QUIZ A — PAGE 48

1. **A** the '**yu**' in yum
2. **B**
3. **D**
4. **C** ㅈ
5. **C** 3
6. **B** 4
7. **C**
8. **A C F G**
9. **B**
10. **D** the '**g**' in gum

QUIZ B — PAGE 78

1. **D** the '**ye**' in yes
2. **B** 11
3. **B G H**
4. **C** 키위
5. **A** the '**wee**' in week
6. **A** 6
7. **B**
8. **D**
9. **C** computer
10.

QUIZ C — PAGE 90

1. **B** Like '**k**' in dock
2. **C** 11
3. **D**
4. **B** 7
5. **C** Like '**l**' in laugh
6. **B** Like '**k**' in dock
7. **A** [말께]
8. **B**
9. **D** [갑슬]
10. **C** Like '**l**' in laugh

QUIZ D — PAGE 122

1. 4 = 사
   9 = 구
   2 = 이
   7 = 칠
2. 8 = 팔
   3 = 삼
   5 = 오
   1 = 일
3. 23 = 이십삼
   69 = 육십구
   16 = 십육
   38 = 삼십팔
4. **C** 2/3
5. **D** 월요일
6. **A** 십일월
7. **A** blue
8. 416 = 사백십육
   812 = 팔백십이
   321 = 삼백이십일
9. 540 = 오백사십
   199 = 백구십구
   704 = 칠백사

Part 9

PRACTICE PAGES
GRID PAPER FOR FURTHER PRACTICE

Part 10

FLASH CARDS
PHOTOCOPY OR CUT OUT & KEEP

ヌ	ネ	ノ
ミ	ム	メ
マ	モ	ヤ
ユ	ヨ	ラ

DIGEUT
디귿

INITIAL d like the 'd' in door
FINAL   t like the 't' in dot

NIEUN
니은

INITIAL n like the 'n' in no
FINAL   n like the 'n' in fun

KIEUK
키읔

INITIAL k like the 'k' in kite
FINAL   k like the 'k' in kite

GIYEOK
기역

INITIAL g like the 'g' in gum
FINAL   k like the 'k' in dock

BIEUP
비읍

INITIAL b like the 'b' in baby
FINAL   p like the 'p' in slap

MIEUM
미음

INITIAL m like the 'm' in mob
FINAL   m like the 'm' in hum

RIEUL
리을

INITIAL r like the 'r' in run
FINAL   l like the 'l' in reel

TIEUT
티읕

INITIAL t like the 't' in tin
FINAL   t like the 't' in not

CHIEUT
치읓

INITIAL ch like the 'ch' in chat
FINAL   t   like the 't' in cat

JIEUT
지읒

INITIAL j like the 'j' in juice
FINAL   t like the 't' in chat

SIOT
시옷

INITIAL s like the 's' in snow
FINAL   t like the 't' in carpet

PIEUP
피읖

INITIAL p like the 'p' in pizza
FINAL   p like the 'p' in nap

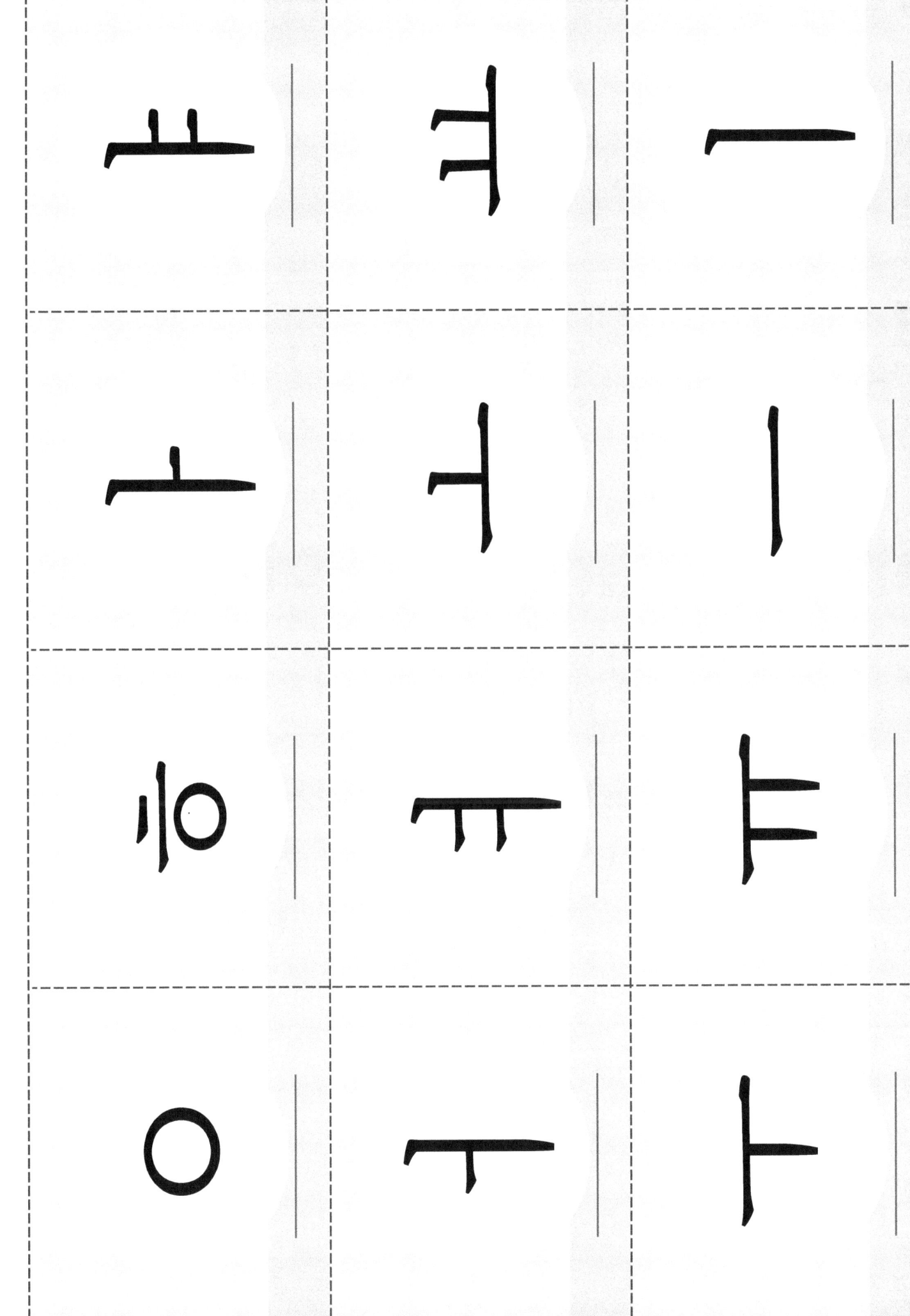

HIEUT

핳
읗

INITIAL **h** like the 'h' in hot
FINAL **t** like the 't' in hot

IEUNG

이
응

INITIAL **silent** placeholder
FINAL **ng** like the 'ng' in sang

'A'

Pronounced like the **'a' sound in father**

'YA'

Pronounced like the **'ya' in yard**
Just as with 'a' but with a soft 'y' sound at the front.

'EO'

Pronounced like the **'u' in bus**
Mouth open in a long tall shape, and keeping your lips still.

'YEO'

Pronounced like the **'yo' in yum**
Just as with 'eo' but with a soft 'y' sound at the front.

'O'

Pronounced like the **'o' in ago**
Mouth open in an O-shape, with your lips kept still.

'YO'

Pronounced like the **'yo' in yoga**
Just like letter 'o' but with a soft 'y' sound at the front.

'U'

Pronounced like the **'oo' in pool**
Rounded lip shape, open mouth with lower mouth coming forward

'YU'

Pronounced like the **word 'you'**
Just as with 'u' but with a soft 'y' sound at the front.

'EU'

Like a disappointed **'eugh'**
'Uh' with wide mouth, corners pulled back, teeth closer together (not closed)

'I'

Pronounced like the **'ee' in sleep**
Wide mouth, teeth closer together (not closed)

며	어	구
규	여	의
배	허	에
배	어	위

'YE'
like the 'ye' in yes
Just as ㅔ with a 'y' sound at the front

'E'
the 'e' in get or hem
Difficult to distinguish from ㅐ

'YAE'
'yeh' like the word 'yeah'
Just like ㅐ with a 'y' sound at the front

'AE'
'eh' almost like the 'e' in egg
Difficult to distinguish from ㅔ

'WI'
the 'we' in week (soft 'w')
'oo-ee' but in a single, smooth sound

'WAE'
'weh' like the we in west
Essentially 'ob-ae' said as a single sound

'WA'
'wa' in Taiwan (soft 'w')
Like 'ob-ab', said as single sound

'OE'
'weh' like the 'we' in wet
Said 'ob-eh' like 'we' in wet & west

SSANG GIYEOK
쌍기역

'UI'
'u-ee', or 'u-wee' (soft 'w')
Like 'eu-ee' but in a single short sound

'WE'
'we' in west or wet (soft 'w')
Like 'o-eb' (hard to distinguish from 외)

'WO'
the 'wo' in wok (soft 'w')
Like 'ub-or' said in short, smooth way

'guh', similar to the 'g' in great
Similar to ㄱ but more forced & tense

| ㄸ | ㅃ | ㅆ | ㅉ |

| SOUND SIMPLIFICATION 받침 | COMPLEX CONSONANTS 겹받침 | ASSIMILATED SOUNDS ㄹ | CARRYING OVER SOUNDS ㅁ아 |

| ASPIRATION EFFECT OF ㅎ | PALATAL EFFECTS OF 이/히 | NASAL ASSIMILATION ㅁ/ㅇ | INCREASING INTENSITY  |

SSANG JIEUT

쌍 지읒

the 'j' in job, with force to start
Sounds similar to ㅈ *(jieut), but tense*

SSANG SIOT

쌍 시옷

a '-s' sound, made with force
Sounds similar to ㅅ *(siot), but tensed*

SSANG BIEUP

쌍 비읍

the 'b' in boy or banana.
Sounds similar to ㅂ *(bieup) but tense*

SSANG DIGEUT

쌍 디귿

the 'd' sound in department
Sounds similar to ㄷ *(digeut) but tense.*

RE-SYLLABIFICATION

Final consonant followed by an initial vowel, **carry sound over**

ㅁ 아 → ㅁ ㅏ
ㅁ ㅇ약

Final ㅇ not carried over, and
Final ㅎ not heard/weak

ㄴ+ㄹ > ㄹ+ㄹ
ㄹ+ㄴ

Creates a **Double 'L'** Sound

But otherwise....

ㄹ+ㄹ > ㄹ

Creates a **Single 'L'** Sound

ㄳ ㄵ ㄽ
ㄺ ㄶ ㄻ
ㄼ ㄾ ㅀ
ㄿ ㅄ

Followed by a Consonant:
Pronounce **FIRST**

Followed by a Vowel:
SPLIT - CARRY 2ND - SAY BOTH
Pronounce **SECOND**

Exceptions apply

Change Pronunciation
as **Final Consonants**

ㄲ ㅋ > ㄱ
ㅌ ㅎ ㅅ > ㄷ
ㅈ ㅊ ㅆ
ㅍ > ㅂ

INTENSIFICATION

ㄱㄷㅂㅅㅈ following 받침
are doubled to ㄲ ㄸ ㅃ ㅆ ㅉ

ㅂㅈ ㅂㅉ 잡지

Final ㅎ only intensifies an
Initial ㅅ, making it a ㅆ

ㄱ+ㄴ/ㅁ > ㄱ=ㅇ
ㅂ+ㄴ/ㅁ > ㅂ=ㅁ
ㄷ+ㄴ/ㅁ > ㄷ=ㄴ

Note: ㄱ+ㄹ > ㅇ=ㄴ

When simplified 받침
meet nasal sounds ㅁ or ㄴ

PALATALIZATION

ㄷ + 이 > 지
ㅌ + 이 > 치
ㄷ + 히 > 치

ㄱ   ㄱ > ㅋ
ㄷ+ㅎ OR ㅎ+ㄷ > ㅌ
ㅂ   ㅂ > ㅍ
ㅈ   ㅈ > ㅊ

New sounds made with certain
letter combinations at speed.

Consonant Sounds
Strengthened by ㅎ

감사합니다
(gam-sa-ham-ni-da)

Thank you

Thank you for choosing our book!

You are now well on your way to learning how to read, write and speak Korean, and we hope that you enjoyed our Hangul workbook for beginners.

If you enjoyed learning Korean with us, we would very much like to hear about your progress in a review

We are always eager to learn if there is anything we can do to make our books better for future students. We are committed to making the best language learning content available! Please do get in touch with us via email if you had a problem with any of the content in this book:

hello@polyscholar.com

POLYSCHOLAR

www.polyscholar.com

© Copyright 2021 Jennie Lee - All Rights Reserved

Legal Notice: This book is copyright protected. This book is only for personal use. The content contained within this book may not be reproduced, duplicated, or transmitted without direct written permission from the author or the publisher. You cannot amend, distribute, sell, use, quote, or paraphrase any part of the content within this book, without the consent of the author or publisher.

www.ingramcontent.com/pod-product-compliance
Lightning Source LLC
Chambersburg PA
CBHW060416010526
44107CB00006B/711